THE IRISH SLAVES

Rhetta Akamatsu

TABLE OF CONTENTS

IRISH SLAVES: THE BACKGROUND HISTORY

At the beginning of the 17th Century, in the reign of James I of England, England faced a problem: what to do with the Irish. They had been practicing genocide against the Irish since the reign of Elizabeth, but they couldn't kill them all. Some had been banished, and some had gone into voluntary exile, but there were still just too many of them.

So James I encouraged the sale of the Irish as slaves to the New World colonies, not only America but Barbados, the West Indies, and South America. The first recorded sale of Irish slaves was to a settlement along the Amazon in South America in 1612. However, before that there were probably many unofficial arrangements, since the Irish were of no importance and details of how they were dealt with were not deemed necessary.

In addition, Irish slaves were also sold to other countries. In *The Many-headed Hydra: The Hidden History of the Revolutionary Atlantic,* by Peter Linebaugh and Marcus Rediker, it is reported that a thousand Irish slaves were sold to Sweden in 1610. Later, in the 1800's, many were sent to Australia, as we will discuss later in the book.

From the 8th to the 11th century, the Irish were often captured by Vikings and sold to Spain, Scandinavia and Russia, according to Ruth Mazo Karras' book, *Slavery And Society in Medeivel Scandinavia.* But the Vikings were not specifically targeting the Irish. They took slaves from Britain, Scotland, Ireland, France, and everywhere else that their ships took them. The English, on the other hand, deliberately targeted the Irish, and the Scots, because at that time there was no distinction made between the Irish and the Scots.

The English had an old and virulent contempt for the Irish. In 1574, when an expedition led by the Earl of Essex slaughtered the entire population of Rathlin Island in Ulster, totalling over 600 people, one of the members of the expedition, Edward Barkley, wrote that "How godly a deed it is to overthrow so wicked a race the world may judge: for my part I think there cannot be a greater sacrifice to God." (Quoted by Nicholas Canny in "The ideology of English colonisation from Ireland to America",William and Mary Quarterly, 1973.)

When the English began to target the Irish, women and children were especially vulnerable. Children were snatched up by slavers and carted off to town prisons or workhouses on spurious charges, such as "vagrancy." When the parents finally discovered where they were, if they did, and tried to claim them to take them home, the jailers demanded that they pay for the food the children had eaten while imprisoned. If they couldn't, as was usually the case, the children were then transported and sold as slaves.

In 1641, one of the periodic wars in which the Irish tried to overthrow the English disrule in their land took place. As always, this rebellion eventually failed. As a result, in the 12 years following the revolt, which was known as the Confederation War, the Irish population fell from 1,466,000 to 616,000. Over 550,000 Irishmen were killed, and at least 300,000 were sold as slaves.

The men were not allowed to take their wives and children, of course. The women and children who were left homeless and destitute had to be dealt with, so they were rounded up and sold, too. Sometimes they were sent to prisons or workhouses, and deported from there. Sometimes they were just snatched up, either from the side of the road or from their beds, and spirited away. It is from this time the word "kidnapped" comes into the language.

After the 1649 conquest, Sir William Petty estimated that one-sixth of all Irish men had been shipped away and sold abroad. That made a lot of Irish women and children suddenly very easily available to the slave trade.

These men, women and children were truly slaves, not indentured servants as some have claimed. The so-called indentured servants were another part of the sad story, and we will deal with them later.

And yet even though it did not seem that things could get worse than they were under James I, when Oliver Cromwell assumed control of the English government, they got much worse indeed.

In 1652, Cromwell instigated the Ethnic Cleansing of Ireland. He demanded that all Irish people were to resettle west of the Shannon, in arid, uninhabitable land, or be transported to the West Indies, giving up the lands that they had possessed for many generations. The majority of the Irish refused to relocate peaceably, knowing that they couldn't survive if they did. There was no grazing land for sheep, no viable land to plant crops. These Irish became outlaws on the land that had once belonged to them. Cromwell had to do whatever was necessary to see that they were removed, because their land had been promised to the troops as payment for putting down the Irish rebellion.

The soldiers were encouraged to kill the Irish who refused to move; it was certainly not considered a crime. But it did not take long for Cromwell to realize that the slave trade was so profitable that it was much more lucrative to round them up and sell them. Gangs went out to fill quotas by capturing whoever came across their path; they were so industrious that they accidentally captured a number of French and English and several thousand Scots in the process. By Cromwell's death, at least 100,000 Irish men, women, and children had been sold in the West Indies, Virginia, and New England. The men were generally sold for life if they were political prisoners; the women and children were supposed to be sold for a certain period of years, after which, they were to be free, should they survive that long. For the children, the bondage was generally to be until the age of 21. It was by no means certain that they would survive that long.

The government of England negotiated deals with ships' captains to carry the captives, in which the prisoners were to be sold upon delivery and the captain was to make a good profit from their sale, and return some of the money to the Crown, as in this letter from a slightly later datepreserved by the Immigrant Ships Transcribers Guild, with the original spelling:

Liverpool, England to Yorktown, Virginia
14 January 1716

Virginia-
By his Majestys' Lieutenant Governor &
Commander in Cheif of this
Dominion-
These are to certify that the above Lift of one hundred & Twelve
Rebel Prisoners, Imported into this Colony in the Ship Elizabeth & Ann,
of Liverpool, Edward Trafford Master, was taken (by my order) upon the
arrival of the faid Ship in York River by the officer of the Customs
there, and contains the Names of all the Prifoners Imported in the sd
ship & that besides the said one hundres & twelve persons, the Mafter
did Report that one other Prisoner by name Duncan Mackfale died at sea,

which upon Examination of the other Prisoners
apeared to be true-
Given under my hand at Williamsburgh this
14th day of January 1716-

In *The Reconquest of Ireland,* James Connelly
describes another business arrangement
between the British government and a private
company to supply servants to New England:

Captain John Vernon was employed by
the Commissioners for Ireland to
England, and contracted in their behalf
with Mr. David Sellick and the Leader
under his hand to supply them with two
hundred and fifty women of the Irish
nation, above twelve years and under
the age of forty-five, also three hundred
men above twelve years and under fifty,
to be found in the country within twenty
miles of Cork, Youghal and Kinsale,
Waterford and Wexford, to transport
them into New England." This British
firm alone was responsible for shipping
over 6,400 girls and boys. . .

ABOARD SHIP

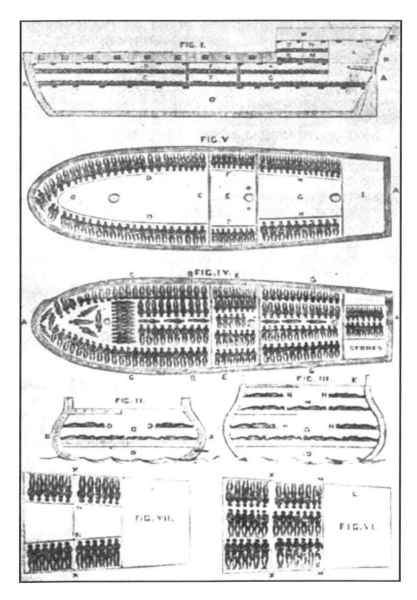

Slave ship. The cargo was carried the same way, whether
black, white, indentured, or enslaved.

Once aboard ship, the chances of actually making it to the new destination were not great.

The conditions of the slaves onboard ship were miserable. No one really cared if they lived or died, as they were cheap and plentiful. One eye-witness described typical conditions thus:

> There is on board these ships terrible misery, stench, fumes, horror, vomiting, many kinds of sea-sickness, fever, dysentery, headache, heat, constipation, boils, scurvy, cancer, mouth rot, and the like, all of which comes from old and sharply salted food and meat, also from very bad and foul water, so that many die miserably . . . . Children from 1 to 7 years rarely survive the voyage.

Marcus Jernigan, writing in "Slavery and the Beginnings of Industrialism in the American Colonies," stated that:

The voyage over often repeated the horrors of the famous 'middle passage' of slavery fame. An average cargo was three hundred, but the shipmaster, for greater profit, would sometimes crowd as many as six hundred into a small vessel...The mortality under such circumstances was tremendous, sometimes more   than half...Mittelberger (an eyewitness) says he saw thirty-two children thrown into the ocean during one voyage.

These conditions did not improve as long as the slavery trade lasted. In the article "The Forgotten Slaves: Whites in Servitude in Early America and Industrial Britain," by Michael A. Hoffman II, he states that as late as 1855, Fredrick Law Olmsted, the premiere landscape artist of his day, was traveling in Alabama and saw black men throwing huge bale of hay carelessly down into the hold of a cargo ship. The hold was filled with white men. Hoffman claims that Olmsted asked about this and was told by a shipworker, "Oh, the niggers are worth too much to be risked here; if the Paddies are knocked overboard or get their backs broke, nobody loses anything."

Hoffman also quotes a study of white slave transport in the Parliamentary Petition of 1659, in which it was reported that the Irish slaves were kept in the hold aboard ship for two weeks before the ship even set sale, and were then chained at the neck and the legs and "all the way locked up under decks...amongst horses."

One account describes a horrible incident on one voyage:

> Every two weeks at sea the [indentured servant] passengers received an allowance of bread. One man and his wife, having eaten their bread in eight days, staggered before the captain and begged him to throw them overboard, for they would otherwise starve before the next bread day. The captain laughed in their faces, while the ship's mate, even more of a brute, gave them a bag of sand and told them to eat that. The couple did die before the next ration of bread, but the captain charged the other passengers

for t e bread the two would have eaten if they had survived."

The crews of these ships were often slaves themselves, "pressed" into service by unscrupulous landlords who drugged them and sold them to ships' captains, or who were freed from debtor's prisons only because a captain chose them as "crew" to serve until their sentence was finished, should they survive. Except for the captain and his staff, these sailors were also routinely kept at near-starvation levels and were beaten ruthlessly over any small cause. Certainly, they were in no condition to show sympathy to their fellow slaves in the hold. Even the captain of one slave ship described the lot of the sailors thus: "There is no trade in which sailors are treated with such little humanity... I have myself seen them when sick, beaten for being lazy till they had died under the blows"

It is an unfortunate fact that those who are brutalized tend to look for someone even weaker to take it out on, so many of those sailors, no doubt, relieved their feelings by being particularly unkind to the human cargo they carried, black or white. Women and children, of course, were especially fair game for the crews and even the captains.

Even in the later days of the trade in white labor, when indentured servitude was the rule rather than actual slavery, and after indentured servitude gave way to contract labor, things did not improve aboard ship.

In the 1840's, during the Potato Famine, when hordes of poor Irish came to America either as indentured servants or to work for, literally, slave wages, they faced terrible times at sea and many did not make it. Conditions were usually worse aboard ship for the Irish at that time than for the African slaves, as the slaves were a more valuable commodity.

Inadequate food, water, and sanitation made ocean crossings dangerous to health and life. In the most disastrous year of all, 1847, about 20 percent of the huge number of immigrants caused by the famine died en route to America or upon landing. This was about 40,000 dead—mostly young people in the prime of life. By comparison, the loss of life among slaves transported from Africa in

British vessels in the nineteenth century was about 9 percent. (Thomas Sowell, *Ethnic America*.)

THE WEST INDIES

THE WEST INDIES

In 1625, the King issued a proclamation that all Irish political prisoners were to be transported to the West Indies and sold as slave labor to the planters there. At that time, he sold 30,000 Irish slaves to the New World. By the mid 1600's, most of the slaves in Montserrat and Antigua were Irish. In 1637, a census showed that 69% of the inhabitants of Monsarrat in the West Indies were Irish slaves.

The Irish had a tendency to die in the heat, and were not as well suited to the work as African slaves, but African slaves had to be bought. Irish slaves could be kidnapped if there weren't enough prisoners or former inhabitants of workhouses, and of course, it was easy enough to make Irish prisoners by manufacturing some petty crime or other. This made the Irish the preferred "livestock" for English slave traders for 200 years.

A document known as *The Edgarton Manuscript,* in the British Museum, which dates from 1652, stated:

It may be lawful for two or more justices of the peace within any county, citty or towne, corporate belonging to the commonwealth to from tyme to tyme by warrant cause to be apprehended, seized on and detained all and every person or persons that shall be found begging and vagrant.. in any towne, parish or place to be conveyed into the Port of London, or unto any other port from where such person or persons may be shipped into a forraign collonie or plantation.

To be vagrant, all a person had to do was to be outside his or her home. Children, especially, were prone to be "vagrant" if they wandered too far in their play.

In 1655, according to an article in *Catholic World,* Volume 8, which was published in 1869 by the Paulist Fathers, all of the Irish in the town of Lackagh in the county of Kildare were seized. There were 41 citizens; 4 were hanged and the rest were transported to be sold as slaves, including two priests.

In the 1650's, England captured Jamaica from the Spanish, and suddenly had a huge island to populate and make profitable. At first, the plan was to take some of the Irish slaves from Barbados and offer them freedom and 30 acres of land to work tif they would stay there. But the planters in Barbados did not like that plan at all. They complained about not having enough slaves to work the sugar plantations as it was. Some of them did take their slaves and move to Jamaica, where they were given land. But there were still not enough workers. So then Cromwell fell back on his usual strategy and sent his "man-catchers" to round up some more Irish to transport.

In 1656, Cromwell's Council of State ordered 1000 Irish girls and 1000 Irish boys to be rounded up and transported to Jamaica and sold as slaves to the English planters there. This is one of the few official records of slave activity, as most was unrecorded. Henry Cromwell wrote to an official in Jamaica, "Though we must use force in taking them up...it is not in the least doubtful that you may have as many of them as you see fit."

Kathy Miller, in *Emigrants and Exiles: Ireland and the Irish Exodus to North America,* records that, in 1669, an honest agent, Robert Southwell, was unable to convince Irish Catholics to enter service in South Carolina even for generous wages, because, he said, "...they have been so terrified with the ill practice of them to the Caribdn Ileands, where they were sould as slaves, that as yet they will hardly give credence to any other usage..."

Treatment of the slaves there was the same as treatment on other plantations: brutal. At Historyjournal.ie in an article entitled "Irish Slaves in Jamaica," this description given by a visitor to a Jamaican plantation in 1687 of the punishment for striking an owner is recorded: "They are nailed to the ground with crooked sticks on every limb and then applying the fires by degrees from the feet, burning them gradually up to the head, whereby their pains are extravagant".

After Cromwell died in 1660, the Irish briefly hoped that the restoration of the monarchy would relieve their situation and stop the slave trade, but this was not to be. When he realized how profitable the slave trade was, Charles II quickly chartered the Company of Royal Adventurers in 1662. Later, the name was changed to the Royal African Company. Through the Company, Charles II, the Queen Dowager and the Duke of York entered into a contract to supply at least 3000 slaves annually to their chartered company. The use of the Irish as a source allowed them to far surpass that number. With slavery an accepted practice of not only nobility but the royal family itself, there was no hope for relief for the Irish who either could die of starvation at home, in a workhouse or prison, on a ship chained in a hold, or in a strange land, where they would also be beaten, worked beyond exhaustion, exposed to tropical diseases, and, in the case of the women, probably raped. To live free was a rare thing for any Irish person of that time.

There are records of Irish sold as slaves in 1664 to the French on St. Bartholomew, and it is well known that English ships on the way to the Americas typically stopped in Ireland to pick up a cargo of Irish to sell along with their other cargo well into the 18th century.

As impossible as it seemed, things became even harder and more difficult for the already beleaguered Irish in 1695, with the passage of the Penal Laws, meant to punish Irish Catholics for their support of the Stuarts against James II of England. In *The Great Hunger; Ireland 1845-1849,* Cecil Woodham-Smith explains the meaning and results of these laws. A contemporary tellingly wrote that the laws had the express purpose of reducing the Irish Catholics to 'insignificant slaves, fit for nothing but to hew wood and draw water.' Irish Catholics could not vote, hold office, or purchase land. Upon the death of the head of the family, their estate was to be divided among all the sons of the family, unless the eldest became Protestant, when he would inherit everything. Catholics could not attend school or send their children away from Ireland to attend school. Practicing Catholicism was a crime, and to be a priest was illegal and highly dangerous. The stage was set for mass disenfranchisement, loss of land, impoverishment, followed by arrest either for being homeless or stealing in order to survive, or for being discovered practicing your faith. Arrest could easily be followed by sentence to exile and slavery. Edmund Burke described the Penal Laws as "a machine as well fitted for the oppression, impoverishment and degradation of a people, and the debasement in them of human nature itself, as ever proceeded from the perverted ingenuity of man." Thus, at this time in history, it was the Irish Catholics who were most likely to become slaves.

Here, from Seumas McManus' *The Story of the Irish Race,* is a summary of all the ways in which the Penal Laws forced the Irish into a life of crime, leading thousands to be arrested and shipped away as criminals or vagrants to become slaves in the West Indies, Barbados and the Colonies:

- The Irish Catholic was forbidden the exercise of his religion.
- He was forbidden to receive education,
- He was forbidden to enter a profession.
- He was forbidden to hold public office.
- He was forbidden to engage in trade or commerce.
- He was forbidden to live in a corporate town or within five miles thereof.

- He was forbidden to own a horse of greater value than five pounds.
- He was forbidden to purchase land.
- He was forbidden to lease land.
- He was forbidden to accept a mortgage on land in security for a loan.
- He was forbidden to vote.
- He was forbidden to keep any arms for his protection.
- He was forbidden to hold a life annuity.
- He was forbidden to buy land from a Protestant.
- He was forbidden to receive a gift of land from a Protestant.
- He was forbidden to inherit land from a Protestant.
- He was forbidden to inherit anything from a Protestant.
- He was forbidden to rent any land that was worth more than thirty shillings a year.
- He was forbidden to reap from his land any profit exceeding a third of the rent.
- He could not be guardian to a child.
- He could not, when dying, leave his infant children under Catholic guardianship.
- He could not attend Catholic worship.
- He was compelled by law to attend Protestant worship.
- He could not himself educate his child.
- He could not send his child to a Catholic teacher.
- He could not employ a Catholic teacher to come to his child.

- He could not send his child abroad to receive education.

These Penal Laws stayed in effect, for the most part, until the 1820's!

Many other laws had been passed in the 1600's to make sure that the Irish stayed impoverished and were not able to do anything other than agricultural tasks, mainly consisting of herding sheep and growing potatoes in the hard, rocky soil they were confined to. This led directly to the famine in the mid-1800's, when a blight caused the potato crops to be wiped out and the people had nothing to eat, being forced in many cases to become indentured servants, go to the workhouses (from which they were often transported), or starve, as we will see later in this book.

The laws passed in the 1600's stated that the Irish, who were skilled craftsmen, could not import any arts and crafts, cloth, wool, linen, beef, pork, butter, cheese, silk, tobacco, fish or glass. As for trade with the Colonies, the laws made it illegal for them to import'"'anything except horses, servants, and victuals." Even those few Irish who had horses or victuals to import to the Colonies could only do so after the goods had landed in England and paid all English duties and taxes first. This meant, that for most Irish people in desperate need, the only thing they could import to the Colonies was themselves, so if they were not arrested and sent involuntarily away, they were easily persuaded by desperate need to sign any sort of agreement that would get them to the Colonies, even if it meant abject servitude and a near-total lack of rights for a number of years.

No wonder the English claimed the Irish were ignorant, wild, unruly savages: They went to a tremendous amount of effort to try to keep them that way, in order to keep them from competing with or rebelling against England.

English Cartoonist's Depiction of an Irishman

In 1698, Parliament gave in to pressure and allowed private merchants to get into the slave trade with the West Indies, declaring the practice "highly Beneficial and Advantageous to this Kingdom, and to the Plantations and Colonies thereunto belonging."

In *Slavery: A World History*, Milton Meltzer wrote of this time, "Slave trading was no vulgar or wicked occupation that shut a man out from office or honors. Engaged in the British slave trade were dukes, earls, lords, countesses, knights - and kings. The slaves of the Royal African Company were branded with initials D.Y. for the Duke of York."

In 1701, The Calendar of State Papers, Colonial Series of 1701, reported that there were 25,000 slaves in the West Indies, 21,700 of them white. The majority of these would have been Irish, although there were also Scots and Dutchmen among them. Again, after yet another Irish rebellion in 1798, records show that thousands of slaves were sold to America and Australia. Many of these probably also ended up in the West Indies.

According to "Colonists in Bondage: Indentured Servants in America," by Barbara Bigham, published in *Early American Life* in October, 1979, in 1717, the English government established forced exile from England for criminals, which meant they could be transported freely to the West Indies or the Americas, to be sold as bond servants for no less than seven years. Beginning in 1729 and continuing until 1776, about 70% of the people jailed in the Old Bailey were transported and made slaves, about 30,000 convicts in all, who were guilty of everything from highway robbery to debt or petty theft, or the all-encompassing "vagrancy."

Treatment of the slaves was unbelievably brutal for the entire time that they were held in the West Indies. In a book written in 1932 by Joseph J. Williams, *Whence the "Black Irish" of Jamaica,* he reports that the slaves worked from 6 AM until 6 PM under the eye of an overseer, barefoot, dressed only in shirt and drawers. Their homes were shacks made of sticks and plantain leaves.

In the West Indies, the African and Irish slaves were housed together, but because the African slaves were much more costly, they were treated much better than the Irish slaves. Also, the Irish were mostly Catholic, and Papists were hated among the Protestant planters. An Irish slave was much more likely to endure such treatment as having his hands and feet set on fire for even a small infraction than an African one. While in the Colonies, the planters came to pit the blacks against the whites by giving white servants preferential treatment, the opposite was true in the West Indies.

The one advantage the Irish slaves had over the African slaves was that since they were literate and they did not survive well in the fields, they were often used as house servants, accountents and teachers. But the gentility of the service did not correlate to the punishment for infractions. Flogging was common, and most slave owners did not really care if they killed an easily replaceable, relatively cheap Irish slave. While 900 pounds of cotton seemed a reasonable price for an Irish slave to the English, 900 pounds of cotton still equaled only about 5 pounds, while an African slave would cost about anywhere from 20 to 50 pounds, and thus was more of a financial burden should he or she die than the Irish were. Why, you could kill off four of the Irish for one African!

In 1656, Colonel William Bayne wrote to request an increase in the number of African slaves to the West Indies because, he said, "as the planters would have to pay much more for them, they would have an interest in preserving their lives, which was wanting in the case of (the Irish)…"

Lady Nugent was the wife of the British governor in Jamaica in the 1600's. She wrote in her journal of a rare treat they had given their black slaves, with a very telling comment at the end.

> We treated them with beef and punch, and never was there a happier set of people. All day they have been singing odd songs, only interrupted by peals of laughter; and indeed I must say they have every reason to be content, for they have many comforts and enjoyments. *I only wish the poor Irish were half as well off.*

Parliament did pass an act in 1667, *The Act to Regulate Slaves on British Plantations*, which designated certain acceptable punishments, but it applied only to Christian slaves. The Irish who were Catholic were not considered Christian by the Protestant planters. Indeed, any follower of the Pope was considered the enemy of Christianity, and there were no laws to protect them, even from being beaten to death should the owner so choose.

Naturally, the Irish Catholics were not allowed to observe Mass or any other Catholic ritual. The denial of the right to practice their religion was a very difficult thing for the Irish slaves to bear. They constantly sought to be allowed religious freedom. It is recorded, for instance, in Maurice Lenihan's *History of Limerick,* that ". . in 1650, 25,000 Irishmen sold as slaves in Saint Kitt's and the adjoining islands, petitioned for a priest..." and, indeed, some priests who were among the slaves did conduct secret services such as the Last Rite and christenings, even on pain of death should they be discovered.

The Irish died of heat, misuse and disease. Those who tried to run away were often branded with an "FT" For Fugitive Traitor on their foreheads, according to an article in *The Republican News*, an Irish paper, in 1997. That article also recounts how 150 Irish Catholics were rounded up and taken to a small, uninhabited island called Crab and left there to starve, which they did, because they were caught practicing their religion.

The purpose for many of the women and girls who were taken as slaves is clear in the delicately worded passage in Hurloe's State Papers, published in London in 1742: "It was.. a great benefit to the West India sugar planters, who desired men and boys for their bondsmen, and the women and Irish girls... To solace them."

While some of these women were lucky enough to be taken as wives by the planters, and thus avoided many of the indignities faced by other slaves, that was not the usual plight of the female slave. A plantation owner had to be desperate for a wife indeed, to consider one of such low social status as the Irish women were. A much more socially acceptable and even financially rewarding use for those who were older than 12 and less than 45, as was generally requested, was as mistresses and breeders.

A great many planters were quick to start breeding with the Irish slave women, taking them by force and making them their mistresses for as long as they desired. Many of the girls and young women were very pretty and they were all totally at the mercy of their masters, but more than that, while many of the Irish were sold into service for only about 10 years, assuming they survived that long, in the West Indies their children were born slaves for life. The planters knew that most of the mothers would remain in servitude to remain with their children even after their service was technically up, so they would be able to keep both the children and the mothers.

The purpose for which many Irish women were intended in the West Indies is obvious in the statement of Walpole that when women and children were rounded up to sold as slaves, they chose "boys who were of an age to labour, or women who were not past breeding." For the women who were sold as brides for the planters, though they had no choice in the matter, their fate was possibly not worse than many women of their time, who were married off for many reasons without having any say. Women were routinely used for the purposes of their fathers in those days. But a woman with some social stature would still be treated with respect and her needs taken care of.

Many of the slave women were treated just like any animal which could be used to create more stock.

The planters also began to breed the Irish women with the African male slaves to make lighter skinned slaves, because the lighter skinned slaves were more desirable and could be sold for more money. This practice became so common that, in 1681, the English government passed an act "forbidding the practice of mating Irish slave women to African slave men for the purpose of producing slaves for sale." This legislation had nothing to do with morality or racial consideration, but was strictly for monetary interests. The practice was causing the Royal African Company to lose profits, because they could not sell as many slaves if the planters were providing attractive merchandise themselves, or growing their own slaves! (Despite these concerns, from 1680 to 1688, the Royal African Company still managed to sell 249 shiploads of slaves to the Indies and American Colonies, over 60,000 Irish and Africans. The profit was tremendous, despite the over 14,000 lost at sea.)

The slave owners and the slave merchants had their own complicated language for selling slaves, and the term used had great impact on the value of the slave:

Mulatto: the child of a white man and a black woman

Quadroon: the child of a mulatto woman and a white man

Sambo; the child of any mulatto person and a black person

Mustee: the child of a quadroon or Indian female and a white man

Mustiphini: the child of a mustee and a white man

Quintoon: the child of a mustiphini and a white man

Octoroon: the child of a quintoon and a white man

Other slaves were referred to as "Unspeakables:" these were the offspring of any non-white e man with a white woman. That does not mean that breeding of white women with men of color did not happen, but that it was not socially acceptable to mention it in public. It was more "respectable" to breed the females who already had at least a drop of black blood in them than it was the white women themselves.

In Maryland in the 1600's, the courts were engaged for a number of years in the case of "Irish Nell," an Irish slave who was brought from the West Indies and sold to a Maryland planter when her former owner returned to England. The question was whether her children fathered in the West Indies by a black slave were to be slaves or free. Eventually, the children were freed.

Other Irish women were sold into brothels either after some years of breeding or immediately upon arrival, although more of them were sold into brothels in the colonies than in the West Indies, and many of the women sold there were indentured servants rather than technically slaves.. To this day, most people who hear the term "white slavery" equate it to white women sold into sexual bondage, and that is what happened to many Irish women and young girls. In 1833, George Loveless, early Union leader in England, who was transported to Australia (known as New South Wales at that time) for his work, wrote,

England has for many years been lifting her voice against the abominable practice of negro slavery. Numbers of great men have talked, have laboured and have struggled until at length emancipation has been granted to the black slaves in the West Indies. When will they dream of advocating the cause of England's white slaves?

A sad commentary to the situation is that when indentured servants and slaves in the West Indies and elsewhere who were sold for a certain amount of time were freed, they often bought into the very system that had tormented them, especially in Monseratt. This was especially true in later times, when slavery was nearing its end. In the early 1800's, most of the population was Irish, and many of them were freed Irish Catholics who had bought slaves at rock-bottom prices from planters who were selling out before the new laws took force, and who then made a profit when the government compensated them for having to free their slaves. (*An Irish History of Civilization, Volume 1,* Donald H. Akenson.)

In addition to the last of the indentured servants still serving in the West Indies in the 1800's, in 1849-51, small groups of children were sent to the West Indies by the San Pancreas Poor Laws. These orphaned and abandoned children would not have faced conditions as harsh as the indentured servants, but they were still forced labor with no say over their work or treatment, and they were still working under conditions they were not used to in tropical heat that would have been very hard for them to endure.

Among the black population in Monseratt in the 1800's, the Irish heritage was so great that Gaelic was commonly spoken, and when white Irish sailors visited the port, the black inhabitants told them, tongue-in-cheek, that they didn't look too Irish. Moneratt is still often referred to as "the Emerald Isle," and they stamp the passports of visitors with the shamrock.

BARBADOS

Barbados

All to hell we must sail

For the shores of sweet Barbados

Where the sugar cane grows taller

Than the God we once believed in

Till the butcher and his crown

Raped the land we used to sleep in

Now tomorrow chimes of ghostly crimes

That haunt Tobacco Island

'Twas 1659 forgotten now for sure

They dragged us from our homeland

With the musket and their gun

Cromwell and his roundheads

Battered all we knew

Shackled hopes of freedom

We're now but stolen goods

Darkens the horizon

Blackened from the sun

This rotten cage of Bridgetown

Is where I now belong

- Tobacco Island, Flogging Molly

Barbados was claimed for England by Captain James Powell on May 14, 1625. On February 17, 1627, Captain Henry Powell brought the first English inhabitants ashore, 80 settlers and 10 slaves. They soon stripped the land of jungle and planted crops.

The main crops for the English landowners who settled there were tobacco and cotton. The demand for labor was enormous. Soon, more people with money and good ties to the English government were allotted land in Barbados, and in just a few short years, most of the island was deforested and plantations established. Then, in 1642, sugar cane was introduced into the agriculture of the island by the Dutch. From the standpoint of the plantation owners, this occurred just in time, as world-wide tobacco prices dropped in the 1640's.

All of these crops demanded a tremendous number of workers, and these workers were either indentured servants or "criminals" who were consigned to labor for a certain number of years, either voluntarily or, more often, against their will. They were political prisoners, the former inhabitants of debtors' prisons or workhouses, vagrants, children, and people who were kidnapped from their homes, sometimes even from their beds. Some of them had been tricked into signing papers they could not read and did not understand. Either way, once they reached Barbados, they were all the same and all imminently disposable, cheap and easily replaced if they died of overwork, disease, malnutrition or misuse. The practice of sending unwilling Irish and other helpless victims to Barbados was so common and widespread that the term "barbadosed" became part of the common language of the 1600's and 1700's.

Much of this labor was Irish. Father John Grace, who moved surreptitiously among the Irish Catholics, claimed that there were actually 12,000 Irish people in Barbados. Official records claim that there were 8,000 slaves in 1669, of which there was 'a great part Irish, derided by the black slaves as "white slaves" or 'white niggers.'

To illustrate how cheap Irish labor was, Annu reports that when the *Angel,* a ship bound for Virginia, was hit by a storm, the loss statement reported: "Amongst the goods saved were three servants valued at £30 who were disposed of in Barbados."

Cromwell sent many of the Irish his men did not kill to Barbados. After wiping out the entire garrison at Drogheda in 1649, Cromwell stated, ""I do not think 30 of their whole number escaped with their lives. Those that did are in safe custody in the Barbados."

In that same year, Irish slaves in Barbados revolted. The revolt failed, and they were hanged, drawn and quartered. Then their heads were cut off and impaled on pikes and displayed as a warning to other slaves who might be tempted to try to gain freedom.

In 1655, the article from the *Catholic World* of 1869 previously cited in the chapter on the West Indies cites a letter from the Commissioners to the Governor of Barbados, telling him that a ship was on the way with a cargo of Irish who had been "deprived of their lands and seized for not transplanting," including three priests. While it appears the priests were to be sold for a number of years, the letter specifically requested that the priests "be so employed that they may not return again, where that sort of people are able to do so much mischief, having so great an influence over the popish Irish." In other words, see that they are worked to death.

Cromwell had decreed that Irish Catholics were forbidden to attend Catholic services. Many priests were transported and sold as slaves. Any Catholic in Ireland who refused to attend a Protestant service could be fined, and if that person could not raise the money, he would be transported and sold as a slave in Barbados. Corrupt officials often helped the slavers out by offering sections of the population to merchants for their own profit: many of the inhabitants of Galway were sold in this manner, and in 1653, the English Lord who had control of County Cork, Lord Broghill, sold 250 men and 300 women to the merchants Leader and Selleck., according to *White cargo: the forgotten history of Britain's White slaves in America*, by Don Jordan and Michael Walsh.

It was common practice for the slavers to take people from their beds at night. W.E.B. DuBois noted that "Even young Irish peasants were hunted down as men hunt down game, and were forcibly put aboard ship, and sold to plantations in Barbados."

At this time, Cromwell's son, Henry, also rounded up 1,000 "Irish wenches" to be sold in Barbados, and 2,000 Irish boys between the ages of 12 and 14.

"Who knows," he wrote, "but it might be a means to make them Englishmen." Making them English or Christian (Protestant) was often the excuse for selling these Irish Catholics into slavery, entirely overlooking the fact that they would probably die or suffer fates worse than death before that happened, especially all of those "Irish wenches." Did he think they would all be cooks and housekeepers?

Among the slaves, it is estimated that about 200 of them were Irish priests. In Bridgetown, there was a bridge which was called "The Priests' Bridge." The legend is that priests were forced to build it, and then were thrown over the parapet and drowned, as reported in the *Irish Monthly*, Volume 30, published in 1902. Certainly, the legend may be true, as, as we have seen that the priests were singled out for cruel treatment because of their great influence over the Catholic Irish.

Many of these Irish slaves had been in poor shape even before being transported, having been jailed for being poor, homeless, "shiftless," and "idle" vagabonds. They were in dreadful conditions there, and they were taken from there to at least equally dreadful conditions in Barbados. It could be questioned whether they and other prisoners were worse off in Barbados, no matter how appalling their treatment. Far worse were those who were kidnapped, tricked or taken from their beds to be brought to the harsh conditions and hard labor that awaited them. If they were not kidnapped or thrown into jail for false crimes, they were tricked into debt and then transported, or plied with food and drink and convinced to sign papers they could not read and did not understand, and then held captive until the ship's arrival when they were "stored" in the hold.

Upon arrival, these slaves were often brutally whipped before they were even put to work to make sure that they understood their station and as a warning of what would happen if they tried to escape. They were then usually branded with the initials of the owner, on the forearm for the women and the buttocks for the men.

The governor of Barbados wrote, in 1665 and with no apparent sense of shame that the Irish worked all day "in the parching sun without shirt, shoe, or stocking", and were "domineered over and used like dogs."

Up until the mid-1600's, the population of Barbados was overwhelmingly white. In 1627, only 3% of the people on the island were black. By 1643, it was still 86% white. In the 1670's, the high mortality rate among the white slaves and the formation of Dutch and Sephardic companies to provide black slaves led to a drastic increase in the black population, so that by 1684, the percentage of black inhabitants was 66% and by 1786, 79%. This led to many social and cultural changes in the island and for the indentured servants on the island as well. After this point, the owners found new uses for their white slaves, particularly the women. Significantly, according to BBC History, during the last decades of the 17th century, there were more women than men both among the white slaves and the black.

Ruins of slave cottage in Barbados

Sometimes, the Irish who worked in the fields were given mulatto or black overseers who very often took great pleasure in treating them cruelly. According to O'Callaghan:

> The mulatto drivers enjoyed using the whip on whites. It gave them a sense of power and was also a protest against

their white sires. White women in particular were singled out for punishment in the fields. Sometimes, to satisfy a perverted craving, the mulatto drivers forced the women to strip naked before commencing the flogging and then forced them to continue working all day under the blistering sun. While the women were weeding in the fields in that condition, the drivers often satisfied their lust by taking them from the rear.

This forced rape of the poor women was not frowned upon by many of the masters because, of course, if babies resulted they would be slaves themselves and could be kept or sold, and with additional white blood, they would be even more valuable.

As in the rest of the islands of the West Indies and the Caribbean, women were desired by the planters for female companionship, either as wives or mistresses, but also for breeding purposes, because their children, fathered either by the masters or by other slaves, black or white, would be born slaves. This served the purpose of keeping both the children and the mothers working on the plantations, as the mothers would often not leave the children even after they were freed.

Due to yellow fever, malaria, overwork and maltreatment, between 33% and 50 % of the indentured servants in Barbados died before the reached the end of their sentence of servitude.

The slaves were called "red-legs" and "white trash" by the owners. The term "Redleg" is often said to be due to the effect of the tropical sun on the fair skin of the poorly clothed servants, but it was already a term in use at the time for Irish military men, and Sir Edmund Spencer referred to the Irish as "Red-Shankes" in his *A vewe of the present state of Irelande*, published in in 1598 Nevertheless. the fair-skinned Irish did suffer horribly from the heat.

If the white slaves did manage to survive their indenture, possibly because they were house servants rather than field servants, after freedom they were either compelled to continue to work for the plantation owners after "freedom" or were nearly always the poorest of the poor, sometimes only able to survive due to the charity given them by the black slaves. Even if they were given land as their "freedom dues," they could grow only subsistence crops, as all of the cash crops in Barbados took land and labor.

George Washington visited Barbados in 1751 and stayed for six weeks. The future President of the US, who was himself a slave owner, said at the time," In the cool of the evening we rode in the country and were perfectly enraptured with the beautiful scenery which every side presented our view. The fields of cane, corn, fruit trees in a delightful green.." Without doubt, he never gave a thought to the white and black slaves who kept those fields so green with their sweat and blood.

In 1780, when the population was mostly black, and 60% of the white population were either indentured servants or impoverished former servants, there was a great hurricane. The contempt in which both white servants and black slaves were held by the minority owners is reflected in this contemporary statement following the Great Hurricane of 1780; "Whites and Blacks together, it is imagined (the deaths) to exceed some thousands, but fortunately few people of consequence were among the number".

To this day, many of the inhabitants of Barbardos have Irish surnames, with Gills and Murphys being the most common.

The problem the authorities in Barbados encountered with their white slaves was that the Irish refused to be broken. They rebelled constantly, and they incited rebellion among the black salves as well. By the last decade of the 1600's, they had become so much trouble that African slaves were armed and trained as militia to control both the Irish and their fellow black slaves.

Often, the slave rebellions took place when the plantation owners were already distracted by storms or by pirate raids, which happened frequently. If Irish or black slaves were sent to town for help, they could pass word to other slaves along the way of the plans for attack. Because the Irish were so often involved in instigating and taking part in these rebellions, the free white people in Barbados, who already looked down on anyone who was poorer or owned less land and influence than themselves, felt that this proved that the Irish were "wild" and "no better than savages," which, ironically made them feel even more entitled to treat them as less than human. Nevertheless, the inability to control the "wild Irish" did cause the Irish slave trade to diminish in the late 1700's, as black slaves became cheaper and more available.

THE COLONIES

But the Irish were not only sold in the West Indies and Barbados They were sold in the Colonies, as well. It is important to remember that in the 1600's and most of the 1700's, America was merely an extension of England, loyal British subjects of the King and bound by English law and custom. There was no thought of equality among the classes, no more respect for anyone not English than that found among any other English people. Therefore, when there was a need for labor, the Colonies embraced the same notions of indentured servitude and convict labor as the British settlements elsewhere had found so useful.

Children were especially useful. They were easier to control and they could be bound to service for many years, until they reached the age of 21.

As early as 1618, a law was passed to allow "street children," both Irish and English, to be sent to Virginia.

We are informed that the City of London, by Act of Common Council, have appointed one hundred children out of the Multitudes that swarm in that place, to be sent to Virginia, there to be bound apprentice… there are, among their number divers (children) unwilling to be carried thither, and that the City want authority to deliver, and the Virginia Company to receive and carry these persons against their will. We authorise and require the City to take charge of that service to transport to Virginia all and every of the aforesaid children. (From Child Migration; An Overview andTimeline, National Archives of Australia.)

One hundred children were sent in 1619, one hundred more in 1620, and in 1622, after the Indian Massacre of 350 colonists, 100 more were sent with the reinforcements.

From this point on, the exportation of children was accomplished either by legal means through various Poor Laws, by charitable organizations, or by being kidnapped or spirited away, with those being sent illegally by far the majority.

In the 1650's, over 100,000 Irish Catholic children between the ages of 10 and 14 were taken from their parents and sold as slaves, many to Virginia and New England. Unbelievably but truly, from 1651 to 1660 there were more Irish slaves in America than the entire non-slave population of the colonies!

In 1692, a reporter for an English newspaper, *The Flying Post*, claimed that he saw 200 kidnapped boys being held in the cargo hold of a ship for transportation to the colonies.

However, it was not only children who were sent as slaves to the Colonisin the 1600's. Men and women were sent as well, either as political prisoners or from the workhouses and prisons, or captured and spirited away in the same way that the children were, sometimes right out of their beds.

This was documented in the British newspaper *Argosy* ,in which, on May 6, 1893, Col. A.B. Ellis wrote,;

Few, but readers of old colonial State papers and records, are aware that between the years 1649-1690 a lively trade was carried on between England and the plantations, as the colonies were then called, in political prisoners... where they were sold by auction to the colonists for various terms of years, sometimes for life as slaves.

In 1676, Nathaniel Bacon led a rebellion in Virginia which focused both on a hatred of the Native Americans of the region and a deep resentment of black and white slaves and former slaves and indentured servants against the landowners and masters. The rebellion died when Bacon died of a "bloody flux," but it scared the landowners badly. They thing that scared them was the fact that the black and white slaves had fought together. At that time, the landowners decided that mostly black people would be slaves, and they would be used mainly for the agricultural work, whereas the Irish and other white slaves would be "indentured servants" with the promise of freedom if they survived their indenture. This was deliberately done to cause a rift between black and white free labor, and

for no other reason, certainly not any feeling
on the white landowners that the Irish were in
any way superior to the black slaves.

Despite of these changes in the way they were
treated, Irish prisoners, political and otherwise,
continued to be slaves.. In *Emigrants and Exiles,*
Kerby Miller states that between 1700 and 1775, at
least 10,000 Irish "convicts" were sold to the
Colonies, primarily to Maryland and Virginia. Most
of these were "vagrants and rogues," which meant
some were peddlers, traveling musicians, homeless
people who had been dispossessed from their land,
or petty thieves who may have stolen food or
clothing for themselves or their families. Many
claimed that they had been "stolen in Ireland, by
some of the English soldiers, in the night out of
theyr beds.weeping and crying."

In *Irish Immigrants in the Land of Canaan,* written
and edited by Kerby Miller, Arnold Schrier, Bruce
Boling, and David Doyle, the number of immigrants
is substantially higher. They report that 14,000 were
shipped directly from Ireland in the 1700's, and that
many of the 50,000 shipped from England during
that time were also Irish. Most of the immigrants
shipped from England served 14-year sentences in

the states, mostly on plantations in Maryland and Virginia. Most were males in their teens and early 20's, and most were unskilled and illiterate laborers or craftsmen. This was a time when almost every European immigrant landed in America 'in bondage" and at least 9 out of 10 Irish. While only about 10% of these indentured servants ran away, for the Irish the percentage was much higher.

Thomas Addis Emmet, in *Ireland Under English Rule*, published in 1902, stated that "between 20,000 and 30,000 men and women who were taken prisoner were sold in the American colonies as slaves, with no respect to their former station in life." Richard Hofstadter claims that almost 30,000 "felons" were transported to the colonies as servants in the eighteenth century, about two-thirds of whom went to Virginia and Maryland.

Other starving and homeless people were lied to or tricked into signing documents agreeing to be sold in America for a term of years to work as slave labor, and these became indentured servants. Agents, called "spirits," would search for the hungry, dusty souls struggling to survive, and offer them dinner and drink. The agent would then cajole the individual into signing a paper which he or she could not read, hustle the victim to a safe place where, with others, they would be held without a chance of escape until a ship was available. Of course, any drunk on the street was even easier prey. Children were easiest of all. They could either be bribed with sweets or simply overpowered and carried away, and sold until they reached the age of 21.

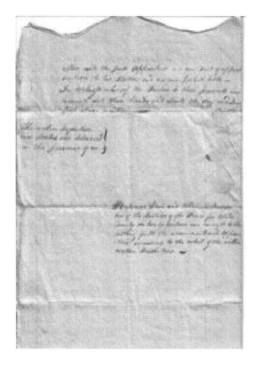

Indenture binding a 4 –year-old 'pauper" to servitude until his 21st year, New York, 1797

Men and women alike, for the entire 17th Century, from 1600 until 1699, there were many more Irish sold as slaves to the Colonies than Africans.

A Dictionary of American History states that between 1700 and 1775, more than 109,000 Irish men, women and children came to the colonies, about 42,000 of them Catholic and the rest Scotch-Irish protestants from around the Ulster area. After 1780, most of the Irish who arrived were Catholic, which was sometimes helpful to them because in places where the Church was established, they would often receive help from the Church, especially if they were indentured and eventually served their time and were free, and sometimes led to even more discrimination, depending on the geographical location.

In *Irish on the Inside: In Search of the Soul of Irish America*, Tom Hayden quotes Thomas Addis Emmett as saying that these Irish "...were sent abroad into slavery in the West Indie, Virginia and New England, that they might thus lose their faith and all knowledge of their nationality, for in most instances even their names were changed." These political prisoners, former homeless, and denizens of workhouses and prisons were often not offered contracts stating that they could work their way to freedom. They were also often branded with the initials of the ship that brought them to be sold. This was a way of breaking the spirit, literally taking away the identity of the person. Denying them the right to practice their religion or any of their cultural rituals was another way of trying to get these new slaves to accept their fate.

When the convicts and indentured servants arrived in the colonies, they were treated much as the later black slaves were treated, as they were lined up for inspection by planters and other prospective buyers who would negotiate for them with the Captain. James Revel, a transported convict wrote in his long narrative poem , "The Poor Unhappy Felons' Sorrowful Account of His Fourtee Years Transportation in Virginia in America":

The women from us separated stood,
As well as we by them to be thus view'd,
And in short time some men up to us came,
Some ask'd our trade, others ask'd our name.

Some view'd our limbs turning us round,
Examining like horses if we were found,
What trade my lad, said one to me,
A tin-man sir. That will not do for me.

Some felt our hands, others our legs and feet,
And made us walk to see if we were compleat.
Some viewed our teeth, to see if they were good,
And fit to chew our hard and homely food.

If any like our limbs, our looks and trades,
Our captain then a good advantage make,
For they a difference make it doth appear,
'Twixt those of seven and those of fourteen years.

Another difference make it doth appear,
Those who have money will have favour shew'd;
But if no cloaths nor money they have got,
Hard is their fate, and hard will be their lot.

At length a grim old man unto me came,
He ask'd my trade, likewise my name,
I told him I a tin-man was by trade,
And not eighteen years of age I said,

Likewise the cause I told which brought me here,
And for fourteen years transported were;
And when from me he this did understand,
He bought me of the captain out of hand.

Of course, there was a great demand for women in the early years of the colonies, and the purpose they were to serve was no secret. In *The Women's History of the World*, Rosalind Miles describes how these women were treated. They were sold, in Jamestown, for "120 pounds of best tobacco" and thus bound to the seller for wife, servant, or mistress for life. Within two years, the price for a woman had rocketed to 150 pounds, and a clerk in London, Miles reports, "forged himself a "Commission to take up yeoman's daughters to serve His Majesty as breeders in Virginia."

The flippant attitude toward the use of women servants and, in some cases men servants, in the writings of one George Alsop, writing in Maryland in 1663, tells us much:

> The Women that go over into this Province as Servants, have the best luck here as in any place of the world besides; for they are no sooner on shoar, but they are courted into a Copulative Matrimony, which some of them (for aught I know) had they not come to such a Market with their Virginity, might have kept it by them untill it had been mouldy, unless they had to let it out by a yearly rent to some of the Inhabitants of Lewknors-lane [a disreputable neighborhood in London]... Men have not altogether so good luck as Women in this kind, or natural preferment, without they be good Rhetoricians, and well vers'd in the Art of perswasion then (probably) they may ryvet themselves in the time of their Servitude into the private and reserved favour of their Mistress, if Age speak their Master deficient." (George

Alsop, A Character of the Province of
Maryland (1666)

Even those women who were not sold either
to be a wife or a mistress, or, in other cases,
into brothels or other forms of prostitution,
were helpless and easy targets for many
forms of maltreatment.

The last woman killed as a witch during the famous
Massachusetts witch trial, which took place in
Boston in 1688, was an elderly Irish slave woman
named Anne Glover. She had been captured by
Cromwell's men and sold as a slave in the 1650s.
Even after many years, while Anne could recite the
Lord's Prayer in Irish and Latin, a d proved this
during interrogation, she spoke very little English
She and her daughter were working in the
household of John Goodwin, when 4 of Goodwin's
5 daughters got sick. The doctor, not being able to
pinpoint a cause, suggested that it must be
witchcraft. As so often happened, at this point a
teenage girl offered the condemning evidence,
claiming she became ill after seeing Anne's
daughter stealing laundry.

"Goody" Glover was easy prey for the witch hunters, since she was elderly, helpless, and foreign. Cotton Mather himself bragged of visiting this poor woman in jail and "interviewing" her about her religious beliefs and the 'sins' she had committed. He used an interpreter to put the questions to her and torture to extract the answers he needed to see her hanged. One of the tests, for example, was whether or not Glover could recite the Lord's Prayer. As mentioned above, she could, and did, recite it in Gaelic and Latin, but since she did not speak English, she could not recite it in that language, which, to Mather, was the only one that counted, and thus she was condemned. Mather recorded the details in his *Memorable Providences, Relating to Witchcrafts and Possessions*, published in 1689.

Men, women and children alike were not only working as indentured servants in the 17th and 18th centuries, but were still doing so well into the late 1800's. Not all of them were misused or subjected to sexual abuse. Some were treated decently and merely had to work hard for no pay until they had done their time. Those were the lucky ones, and there numbers were not few. However, far more suffered in various degrees during their servitude.

Female indentured servant on a Kentucky farm, 1800's

Elizabeth Dolan, who was a domestic servant in the 1800's, is quoted in *Early Immigrant Letter Stories* as complaining about "hard mistresses" who "want girls on tap from six in the morning to 10 or 11 at night" and "boss... you everlastingly" "Whatever you do don't go into service," she advised..you'll always be prisoners and always be looked down upon".

Few indentured servants or even slaves, no matter their age or sex, were treated as badly outside of the West Indies and Barbados as they were there, and even on the plantations where the Irish slaves and servants worked very hard indeed and often were very badly used, they were seldom treated as badly as they were in the islands, and it would be wrong to imply that they were, In the colonies, some, especially those with skills or those children apprenticed to skilled workers, were treated very fairly and at the end of their labors had gained skills that helped them to get ahead in life, and some were treated generously when it came time for "freedom dues," and were given a bit of land and the means to support themselves, particularly the men. What happened to the women is less clear. Either they married or they stayed in service as domestics, for the most part. Those who had been sold into prostitution, of course, seldom escaped.

Whether the majority of them were treated fairly or not, it was with these early Irish slaves that the template was formed for the later treatment of all English slaves, black and white. The punishments, laws for handling runaways, and general rules for owning human property evolved from the treatment of white, mostly Irish slaves. And except for a few extra provisions for legal recourse and the hope of future freedom, the indentured slaves were handled very much the same. They could be transferred as property during their time of service, they could be beaten, they could be forbidden to work outside of their master's land or receive outside wages, they were forbidden to marry, and if they ran away they could be hunted down, brought back, and have their time of service extended.

In the 1600's, the mistreatment of slaves in the colonies, and the number of those who died or ran away, was so great that Parliament passed a law:

> Whereas the barbarous usage of some servants by cruell masters bring soe much scandall and infamy to the country in generall, that people who would willingly adventure themselves hither, are through feare thereof diverted, and by that meanes the supplies of particuler men and the well seating of his majesties country very much obstructed, Be it therefore enacted that every master shall provide for his servants compotent dyett, clothing and lodging, and that he shall not exceed the bounds of moderation in correcting them beyond the meritt of their offences; and that it shalbe lawfull for any servant giving notice to their masters (haveing just cause of

complaint against them) for harsh and bad usage, or else of want of dyett or convenient necessaries to repaire to the next commissioner to make his or their complaint, and if the said commisioner shall find by just proofes that the said servants cause of complaint is just the said commissioner is hereby required to give order for the warning of such master to the next county court where the matter in difference shal be determined, and the servant have remedy for his grievances. (October 1670)

This law left much room for interpretation, of course, as to what was competent diet, clothing, and lodging, what punishment went beyond the bounds of "moderate," and so on. The law allowed indentured servants who had a complaint against their master to take the matter to law, but they were required to make up the time they missed while in court, usually two days for every one day missed, and it was rare for the courts to find against the masters.

IN 1623, an indentured servant named Richard Frethome, wrote this letter home (printed here in with the original wording and spelling);

…, this is to let you understand that I your Child am in a most heavie Case by reason of the nature of the Country is such that it Causeth much sicknes [including scurvy and "the bloody flux"] . . . and when wee are sicke there is nothing to comfort us; for since I came out of the ship, I never at anie thing but pease, and loblollie (that is water gruell)[.] as for deare or venison I never saw anie since I came into this land there is indeed some foule, but Wee are not allowed to goe, and get yt, but must Worke hard both earelie, and late for a messe of water gruell, and a mouthfull of bread, and beife[.] a mouthfull of bread for a pennie loafe must serve for 4 men which is most pitifull if you did knowe as much as I, when people crie out day, and night. . . . I have nothing at all, no not a shirt to my backe, but two Ragges nor no Clothes, but one poore suite, nor but one paire of shooes, but one paire of stockins, but one Capp, but two bands, my Cloke is stollen by one of my owne fellowes, and to his dying hower would not tell mee what he did with it [although some friends saw the "fellowe" buy butter and beef from a ship, probably purchased with Frethorne's cloak]. . . . but I am not halfe a quarter so strong as I was .., and all is for want of victualls, for I doe protest unto you, that I have eaten more in a day at home than I have allowed me here for a Weeke. . . . (Servants, Slavery, Abolition, and Emancipation: Indentured Servitude, Slavery and Freedom in the United States" by Joyce A. Hansen)

Revel, in his "Sorrowful Account," gives this description of how he and other servants and slaves were treated at his Master's plantation in Virginia:

A canvas shirt and trowzers me they gave,
A hop sack frock in which I was a slave,
No shoes or stockings had I for to wear,
Nor hat nor cap my head and feet were bare.

Thus dress'd, into the field I next did go,
Among tobacco plants all day to hoe,
At day break in the morn our work begun,
And lasted till the setting of the sun.

My fellow slaves were five transports more,
With eighteen negroes which is twenty four,
Besides four transport women in the house,
To wait upon his daughter and his spouse.

We and the negroes both alike did fare,
Of work and food we had an equal share,
And in a piece of ground called our own,
The food we eat first by ourselves is sown.

No other time to us they will allow,
But on a Sunday we the same must do,
Six days we slave for our master's good,
The seventh is to produce our homely food,

And when we a hard day's work have done,
Away unto the mill we must be gone,
'Till twelve or one o'clock a grinding corn,
And must be up by day light in the morn.

And if you get in debt in debt with any one,
It must be paid before from thence you come,
In publick places they'll put up your name,
As every one their just demands may claim.

....

At last it pleased God I sick did fall,
But I no favour could receive at all,
For I was forc'd to work while I could stand,
Or hold the hoe within my feeble hand.

Much hardship then I did endure,
No dog was ever nursed so before,
More pity then the negro slaves bestow'd,
Than my inhuman brutal master show'd.

After black slaves began to be brought in from Africa, the way that Irish and other white servants were treated and the way African slaves were treated began to change, as we have seen, and there was some superficial improvement in the treatment of the Irish, although the attitude toward the Irish "servants" and the black slaves was very similar for two hundred years, as shown in this newspaper *ce,* Marc Aronson notes that black people were often referred to as "smoked Irish" and the Irish as "blacks turned inside out."

However, gradually more and more masters began to see an advantage to creating differences between the black and white "servants," giving the whites roles as overseers or slightly preferential treatment, separating them into different living quarters, and encouraging the white servants to feel superior to the black slaves, so that they would not work together to rebel against the masters and their families, thus setting the stage for hundreds of years of racial tension and trouble among people whose histories had so much in common.

The Ignorant Vote—Honors Are Easy.

Newspaper comparison of blacks and Irish

THE SPECIFIC CASE OF INDENTURED SERVANTS

Indenture certificate signed with an X by Henry Meyer in 1738

Let us look at the nature of indentured servitude, especially as it applied to the Irish

Some scholars have tried to claim that the Irish workers in the West Indies and the colonies were not slaves, but indentured servants, and that that was not the same thing, that all of them had entered into a contract to work for a certain number of years in return for passage. Some of them did do this, especially in the colonies during later years. They wanted so badly to come to America that they bartered their services willingly in return for passage, usually agreeing to work for 4 to 7 years. However, during the 1600's, the vast majority of the Irish in the West Indies and the colonies were sold, in the same way as the Africans were. An Irish slave was more valuable to the English than a free Irish person, bringing as much as 900 pounds of cotton as his or her price. It is true that in some cases, they were sold for a set number of years, but no one cared very much if these terms were honored, and as we will see, the plantation owners quickly found a way to keep many of their slaves for life even after they were technically "free." And the servant had no say whatsoever in any terms of the sale and was owned as truly as any human ever owned another for at least the period of time written in the contract.

Even in the colonies, those who generally opposed slavery were quite willing to take advantage of indentured servants, including those who had been seized and were being sold for a term of years without their consent. In *The Irish relations: trials of an immigrant tradition* by Dennis Clark, the author quotes an Irish exile living near Philadelphia in 1791 who observed of his Quaker neighbors that they did not object to a "brisk trade in Irish slaves."

He wrote: "The members of the society for the abolition of slavery have not the least objection to buying an Irishman or a Dutchman and will chaffer with himself or the captain to get him indented for about the eighth part of the wages they would have to pay a "country-born." '

A typical announcement in the *Virginia Gazette* from the mid-1700's reads: "Just arrived at Leedstown, the Ship Justitia, with about one Hundred Healthy Servants, Men Women and Boys. . . . The Sale will commence on Tuesday the 2nd of April." The only difference in wording between this advertisement and that for black slaves is the word "servant."

This photo is of emancipated slaves, white and black, from Harper's Weekly, January 1864. Some of these children might be the result of mixed blood, and some may have been the offspring of Irish slaves.

So, even when an Irish person was sold for a period of time, he was still enslaved for that amount of time without his consent, and often having never agreed to be seized and transported from his or her home and family. In many cases, these servants were also women and children, completely at the mercy of the captain of the ship as to to whom and where they were sold and then to their masters as to how they were treated. They could be worked as fairly or as cruelly as the owner dared, and no one cared if they died before their time was up. Some masters and mistresses were kindly, of course, and treated their servants in a fair manner, and in many cases the servants learned valuable skills in the course of their indenture, especially in the cities where servants might be apprenticed to carpenters, printers, and the like. However, this was more the exception to the rule when it came to these servants, who, when not mistreated and brutally overworked, were given the bare minimum food, clothing and shelter to survive, few holidays, and no luxuries of any kind. Many masters believed that it was necessary to be harsh in order to "keep the servants in their place."

The low regard in which the indentured servants were held is evident in this letter from Charles Yates to John Hatley Norman, recorded in the *Geography of Slavery* from the University of Virginia:

It is very unlucky that you shoud have addressed your servants to me as I have ever since the unfortunate Bargain I made with Capt. Goosley determined never more to have any concerns with

such cattle - and also yt [that] you
shoud have sent them to this River as
we have been overrun with them
valuable Tradesmen selling by retail
from fifteen to Twenty Pounds on long
creditt - and just now when Mr Thomas
Hodge has a full cargo just arrived - All
I can do for your service will be to
advertise that such Tradesmen as you
mention may be soon expected here and
give Mr Adams on his arrival such
information or advice as may appear
most for your interest..

When indentured servants willingly agreed to work
a number of years in return for passage to America
or the West Indies, it was usually to escape from
extreme poverty or religious or political
oppression. But remember that many of them were
taken by agents known as "spirits," in the same way
that those transported for life were taken and sold.

In *White Servitude,* by Richard Hofstadter, the
actions of the "spirits" are described thus:

The spirits, who worked for respectable
merchants, were known to lure children
with sweets, to seize upon the weak or
the gin-sodden and take them aboard

ship, and to bedazzle the credulous or weak-minded by fabulous promises of an easy life in the New World. Often their victims were taken roughly in hand and, pending departure, held in imprisonment either on shipboard or in low-grade hostels or brothels.

Other indentured servants were "convicts" who had been "pardoned" on the terms that they must agree to be transported to the colonies. Many of these convicts were the inhabitants of debtors' prisons who had been forced into debt they could not pay, or petty thieves who stole food or clothing items. It was against the law in England to impose a punishment of banishment or exile, but offering a pardon in exchange for "voluntary" exile was not. The way the system worked was that a justice or mayor would submit a list of prisoners "worthy" of pardon to the secretary of state, who would approve it; it would then be signed by the king, and the person receiving the pardon would be hauled into court, where he or she would indicate willingness to be transported (having very little choice other than death or starvation.) Often, the merchants who transported these "unsavory persons" received not only the price they could get for selling them into servitude, but money from the British government as well for removing them from the country.

Many of the convicts who were transported to the West Indies, Barbados, and The Colonies, however, had never been legally pardoned, but were simply shipped away to slave status at the word of the authority in charge of whichever hospital, workhouse, or prison the victim was in. (Poor sanitation and unsafe medical practices were not the only reasons that poor people were afraid to go into the hospital for treatment, fearing they might never come out again.)

The state of Georgia is a unique case in the colonies, as it was founded entirely as a "debtors' colony," and all of the earliest settlers were people who were sent there from England because they owed debts they could not pay and were sent to Georgia rather than being sent to the overcrowded Debtors' Prisons in England.

When people came over willingly as "redemptioners," meaning they had signed contracts agreeing to work for a certain period of time (usually between 4 and 7 years,) in exchange for passage to America, it was usually a combination of extreme need and because they had been promised great things. For instance, one pamphlet put out by the Virginia Company promised indentured servants that after their time was served, they would have "houses to live in, vegetable gardens, orchards-and fifty acres of land for themselves and their heirs forevermore."

This pamphlet is quoted in David Olin Relin's article, "Misery," written for *Scholastic Search.* He goes on to explain that the miserable treatment which most indentured servants actually received, having signed away all of their rights for a number of years, was a secret that the company closely guarded. Letters home were rigidly censored, and a law was passed against anyone who should "dare to detract slander or utter unseemly speeches against the company," with the penalty being public execution!

In the colonies, laws were sometimes passed to try to make conditions aboard the ships bringing the servants in less horrible. The laws that Pennsylvania passed in 1750, according to *Wikipedia*, indicate how onerous conditions must otherwise have been:

> According to the statutes of the act, six feet of "Bed Place" was required for every four "whole freights," with a passenger above fourteen years of age constituting a "whole freight." In 1765 the legislature passed a supplemental law that added a "vertical" standard to "horizontal" space specified in the previous act, stipulating three feet nine inches of "Bed Place" at the forepart of the ship and two feet nine inches in the cabin and steerage.

Six feet of space for four grown people, with less than 4 feet of room to sit or stand in, was considered a great improvement. The explanation, of course, is that the laws were not intended to create comfort, but merely to decrease the spread of contagious disease, which not only interfered with the increase in the work force but caused colonists to fear that the disease might spread from the servants to the colonists themselves.

Indentured servants did not fare any better on the trip from England to America, which took at least 7 weeks, than slaves did. Here is a description by Gottlieb Mittelberger, writing in 1754 in *On the Misfortune of Indentured Servant*:

> But during the voyage there is on board these ships terrible misery, stench, fumes, horror, vomiting,   many kinds of sea-sickness, fever, dysentery, headache, heat, constipation, boils, scurvy, cancer,   mouth-rot, and the like, all of which come from old and sharply salted food and meat, also from very   bad and foul water, so that many die miserably.
>
> Add to this want of provisions, hunger, thirst, frost, heat, dampness, anxiety,

want, afflictions and   lamentations,
together with other trouble, as . . . the
lice abound so frightfully, especially on
sick   people, that they can be scraped
off the body. . .

Gottlieb goes on to describe more of the horrors
visited upon women and children during these
voyages:

No one can have an idea of the
sufferings which women in confinement
have to bear with their innocent   children
on board these ships. Few of this class
escape with their lives; many a mother is
cast into   the water with her child as
soon as she is dead. One day, just as we
had a heavy gale, a woman in our   ship,
who was to give birth and could not give
birth under the circumstances, was
pushed through a loop-hole [port-hole]
in the ship and dropped into the sea,
because she was far in the rear of the ship
and could not be brought forward.

Children from 1 to 7 years rarely survive
the voyage. I witnessed misery in no less

than 32 children in our ship, all of whom were thrown into the sea. The parents grieve all the more since their children find no resting-place in the earth, but are devoured by the monsters of the sea.

Often, the ships' captains would advertise skilled indentured servants in advance of their landing, as in this advertisement from the June 10, 1766 Pennsylvania Gazette:

SERVANTS, Just imported in the Ship Hugh and James, Captain McCarthy, from Ireland, and to be sold by CONYNGHAM and NESBITT, A PARCEL of likely young Men, Women, and Boys, among which are, Shoemakers, Taylors, Linen, Worsted and Stockings Weavers, Blacksmiths, Nailors, Carpenters, Joyners, Butchers, Gardiners, Distillers, Millers, a Mill wright, Soap boiler, Sugar boiler, Sadler, Brazier, Upholsterer, Tobacco Spinner, Snuff maker, Currier, Barber, Cooper,

Bricklayer, Breeches maker, and a
Printer.

Gottlieb explains how auctions were carried out on
ships that landed in Philadelphia. He describes how
merchants, businessmen and plantation owners
would come even from long distances to come
aboard ship and choose from the cargo those
servants they thought would best suit their purposes,
and negotiate for their services for a term of years.
Often husband, wives, and children were sold to
different owners and might not see each other again
for many years, if ever. The newspapers were full of
advertisements of people seeking fathers, mothers,
children, brothers, or sisters who had been sold to
different owners. For those whose husband or wife
died at sea, often they were sold for enough money
to make up for the lost spouse, so that their terms of
service were longer or harder than a single person's.
Children who were orphaned on the trip had to
serve until they were 21 years old, no matter how
old they were at the time that they were sold, and
some of these children were as young as 4 or 5
years of age. No one questioned who these orphan
children were sold to or for what, or made
provisions for their safety, although sometimes
requirements were made for a very basic education.
Indeed, in Philadelphia, according to an article titled

"Indentured Servants" written by Karen Mullian of the Albuquerque Genealogical Society, a list of indentured servants bound out by the Guardians of the Poor of the City of Philadelphia shows children as young as 18 months to three years bound as apprentices for as long as 20 years! These children were to learn such trades, according to Millian, as "weaving, shallop fishing, husbandry (farming), housewifery, cordwaining, tobaccanist, shoemaker, joinery (carpentry), tanning, and curriery.". Sometimes the indenture was not that specific, stating only that the child was to learn reading and writing and basic arithmetic, or, in the case of girls, to "read, sew, knit, and spin." What else the children were required to do during their entire growing-up years was up to the masters. (Reading was usually confined to The Bible.).

Hofstadter adds that among the buyers were also agents known as "soul stealers," who "bought packs of immigrants and brutally herded them on foot into the interior where they were offered along the way to ready purchasers." In these cases, no provisions at all were made for the poor servants.

In *Irish-American Historical Miscellany* by John D. Crimmins, published in 1905, these agents are called "soul drivers." Crimmins recounts an amusing tale of one clever young Irishman who managed to trick and elude one of these soul drivers:

> The fellow, by a little management, contrived to be the last of the flock that remained unsold, and traveled along with his owner without companions. One night they lodged in a tavern and in the morning, the young fellow, who was an Irishman, rose early and sold his master to the landlord, pocketed the money, and marched off. Previously, however, to his going he used the precaution to tell the purchaser that his servant, thought tolerably clever in other respects, was rather saucy and given to lying, that he had even presumption at times to endeavor to pass for master, and that he might possibly represent himself so to him. By the time mine host was undeceived, the son of Erin had gained such a start as rendered pursuit hopeless.

Indenture of apprenticeship binding Evan Morgan, a child aged 6 years and 11 months, for a period of 14 years, 1 month. dated Feb. 1,1823, Sussex Co., Delaware.

Even some respectable plantation owners and merchants dealt in indentured servants for sale on the side, as is the case of Captain Charles Ridgely of Maryland;

At one point, in fact, in the 1760's Capt. Charles Ridgely, the consumate businessman, was not only buying indentured servants but selling them as well for a profit. In April 1769, for example, he bought eleven men and nine women from Capt. John Stevenson, paying £12 a man and £9 a woman. Within two months he had sold seven women for sums between £10 and £15 each and eight or nine men for between £17 and £30 making a tidy profit on each individual. (R. Kent Lancaster. Almost Chattel: The Lives of Indentured Servants at Hampton-Northampton, Baltimore County}

A weaver from London who witnessed an auction of Irish slaves in Williamsburg in 1758 gave this description;

They all was set in row, near 100 men
and women and the planter come down
the country to buy . . . I never see such
parcels of poor wretches in my life some
almost naked and what had clothes was
as black as chimney sweeps, and almost
starved by the ill-usage of their passage
by the captain, for they are used no better
than many negro slaves and sold in the
same manner as horses or cows in our
market or fair.

Black historian Lerone Bennett,Jr., in *The Shaping
of Black America*, describes how Irishmen were
sold in North Carolina in the 1640's for 35 barrels
of turpentine.

In 1755, the governor of Maryland wrote that: "The
planters' fortunes here consist in the number of their
servants (who are purchased at high rates) much as
the estates of an English farmer do in the multitude
of cattle."

Even when they survived the journey, many of these people, who were only "indentured servants" and surely not "slaves" did not get to appreciate their survival long,

In 1671, the governor of Virginia estimated that four fifths of the indentured servants died shortly after they arrived, from heat, disease, or ill-use and overwork. They were poorly fed and clothed in many cases and, even when freed, were poverty-stricken and unskilled, with little chance to become more than common laborers, or in the case of the women, cooks, kitchen maids, or prostitutes.

The person, once bought, was not simply consigned to work for his owner for the period of time contracted, but to be that person's slave and do their bidding in all things or be punished just like any other slave, as this Maryland law from the late 1600's indicates:

> Servants refuseing to performe the
> Lawfull Commands of their Masters or
> Mistresses or of their assigne or
> overseer or neglecting to doe the labour

which they ought to doe or unjustly complaining against their Master or Mistress or offending any other wise against their duty or Indenture and the Servant so offending shall be publickly whipped or otherwise Corrected at the discretion of the Judge (Proceedings and Acts of the General Assembly January 1637/8- September 1664}

Irish servants could also be willed to others, just like any other property. In *White Slaves In Americas*, edited by Ogu Eji Ofo Annu, the will of Abraham Coombs of Maryland from 1684 is quoted: "I give and bequeath to my dear and loving wife all my servants, being two boys and one woman servant together with all my stock of hogs."

The constant comparison in writing of these white, mostly Irish, servants to cattle and hogs , or their listing alongside them in wills, inventories, and bills of sale emphasizes the position they held in the eyes of the owners, even those who treated them fairly: they were possessions, to be used to the best advantage of the owner and his family.

The document *Law Case, Master Samuel Symonds against Irish slaves. William Downing and Philip Welch. Salem Quarterly Court. Salem, Massachusetts. June 25, 1661. Records and Files of the Quarterly Courts of Essex County, Massachusetts, vol. II, 1656-1662* sheds a great deal of historical light on the fate of Irish so-called "indentured servants" of that time.

The case begins:

Samuell Symonds, gentleman v. Will. Downing. For absolutely refusing to serve his master, Mr. Simonds, any longer, there being several years yet due, according to the purchase from the shipmaster who brought him over to sell.

Samll. Symonds, gentleman v. Phillip Welch. For absolutely refusing to serve his master, Mr. Simonds, any longer, there being several years yet due, according to the purchase from the shipmaster who brought him over to sell.* Writs, dated, May 15, 1661, signed by Robert Lord, for the court, and served by Theophilus Wilson, constable of Ipswich.

Samuel Symonds,* gent. Complaint to Salem court, June 25, 1661, against his two servants.

Defence of William Downeing and Philip Welch: "We were brought out of or owne Country, contrary to our owne wills & minds, & sold here unto Mr Symonds, by ye master of the Ship, Mr Dill, but what Agreement was made betweene Mr Symonds & ye Said master, was neuer Acted by our Consent or knowledge, yet notwithstanding we haue indeauored to do him ye best seruice wee Could these seuen Compleat yeeres, which is 3 yeeres more then ye use to sell ym for at Barbadoes, wn they are stolen in England. And for our seruice, we haue noe Callings nor wages, but meat & Cloths. Now 7 yeares seruice being so much as ye practice of old England, & thought meet in this place, & wee being both aboue 21 years of age, We hope this honored Court & Jury will seriously Consider our Conditions."

Symonds then states that the deal that he made with the shipmaster was still in force and that because he only had these two servants and they were not working since they were here in court, he and his family were being made destitute since no one was tending the cattle and so on.

John King then testified before the court.

John King deposed that he "with divers others were stollen in Ireland, by some of ye English soldiers, in ye night out of theyr beds & brought to Mr Dills ship, where the boate lay ready to receaue them, & in the way as they went, some others they tooke with them against their Consents, & brought them aboard ye said ship, where there were divers others of their Country men, weeping and Crying, because they were stollen from theyr frends, they all declareing ye same & amongst ye rest were these two men, William Downeing & Philip Welch, and there they were kept, until upon a Lord's day morning, ye Master sett saile, and left some of his water & vessells behind for hast, as I understood." Sworn in court, 26:4:1661, before Hilliard Vern, cleric.

John Downing testified that William Downing and Phillip Welch, with several of their countrymen, were taken up and stolen by the ship master or som one whom he hired. The Ship-master, George Dill, was fain to go away and leave his water and much of his provisions behind for fear the country would have taken them from him. Sworn, June 24, 1661, before Daniel Denison.

John Downing further made oath that he knew that he and three or four others of his townsmen were taken up by force; that he did not know the two parties in question, but they said in the ship that they were stolen and brought by force."

The jury judged that the contract between Mr. Symonds and the captain of the ship was legal, and ordered the two servants to serve two more years, until May 10, 1663. The fact that they were stolen from their beds and transported without their agreement held no weight whatsoever with the court, who held that because they were British subjects and the English government said the captain could transport the men, he had the right to sell them and Symonds had the right to buy them to use as he pleased for whatever term of years he and the captain agreed, and the men had no rights in the matter whatsoever regardless of whether or not they had committed any crime or signed any paper.

Maryland, Virginia, Pennsylvania, Delaware, and New Jersey received more indentured servants than any other colonies in the 17th century. About 80% of all European immigrants at that time were indentured, and while some were "redemptionists" who freely agreed to work a certain number of years to escape from extreme poverty in their home country, and others were not Irish, the majority were either political prisoners, the destitute or homeless (including traveling musicians and peddlers, who owned no land), or those who had been kidnapped and transported, and more of them were Irish than any other ethnicity.

Of all the colonies, Virginia seems to have the most recorded laws concerning indentured servants. For instance, in 1705, the Virginia General Assembly made this declaration:

All servants imported and brought into the Country. . . who were not Christians in their native Country. . . shall be accounted and be slaves...If any slave resists his master. . . correcting such slave, and shall happen to be killed in such correction. . . the master shall be free of all punishment. . . as if such accident never happened.

Remember that the Irish, who were predominantly Catholic, were not considered "Christian" at this time. And "resisting" the master could be so much as a spoken protest, a look, or simply not moving fast enough for the master's liking. So if the servant (not slave!) were then beaten to death or punished in some other way that led to death, the master was not guilty of murder, or even a misdemeanor, but the "accident" might as well never have happened!

Of course, the other colonies also received indentured servants, not all of whom were Catholic. In Boston, in 1730, an announcement appearing in the *Boston News-Letter* for an auction of Irish boys., and a group of women convicts from Belfast was sold in Boston in 1749. As late as 1860, two-thirds of the servants in Boston were Irish. Until the

1840's, most of the Irish indentured servants in Boston were Presbyterians from around Ulster. Only the Penal Codes which cost Irish Catholics their lands and jobs and the potato famine that followed brought Irish Catholics into Boston in the mid-1800's. Many Presbyterian indentured servants from around Ulster and other parts of Northern Ireland also arrived in Delaware and Pennsylvania in the 18th and 19th centuries.

There exist tales of servants being locked up and starved, sent out in thin clothing in freezing weather so that either they died of the cold or caught ill and died, and no one was held in any way accountable for these deaths, other than the "disobedient" servant who brought it on him- or herself.

The average age of the indentured servants who came willingly due to homelessness or poverty or who were kidnapped and "spirited' to America or the West Indies was 15-20, while the "convicts" (many of whom had committed crimes such as stealing a chicken or poaching a rabbit for food) were usually between 20 and 30 years of age. Younger children, however, sometimes appear in the records, some as young as 6 or 7 years of age, and women were always desirable as long as they were past puberty.

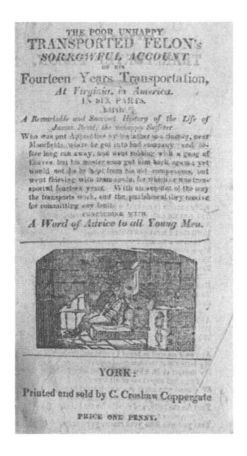

One major difference did exist between the lot of indentured servants in the colonies and in the West Indies, however, and that is that children born to indentured servants in the colonies were free, and not slaves as they were in the West Indies. Of course, this should have been a rare occurrence, happening only in the case of married couples working either in the same house or very near to each other, because indentured servants were forbidden to marry during their servitude. However, it could still become a matter of legal debate. Virginia, in fact, enacted a law in 1662, that if an indentured woman had a child by her master, she had to serve an additional two years as a slave to the church wardens: "That each woman servant gott with child by her master shall after her time by indenture or custome is expired be by the churchwardens of the parish where she lived when she was brought to bed of such bastard, sold for two years."

This, despite the fact that there was no law saying that a master could not force a female indentured servant to have sex with him without facing any penalty, as she was his personal property to do with as he pleased. Masters, of course, were never held accountable.

Even though children born to indentured servants were supposed to be free, this was not the case if the father of the children was a slave. The need for a constant supply of slaves for the labor force caused some plantation owners in the colonies to try to increase their slaves by the same method the West Indies plantation owners often employed, breeding the Irish indentured women to the black slaves. This became so common, that Virginia was forced to make a law about this as well:

> And for prevention of that abominable mixture and spurious issue which hereafter may encrease in this dominion, as well by negroes, mulattoes, and Indians intermarrying with English, or other white women, as by their unlawfull accompanying with one another, Be it enacted by the authoritie aforesaid, and it is hereby enacted, that for the time to come, whatsoever English or other white man or woman being free shall intermarry with a negroe, mulatto, or Indian man or woman bond or free shall within three months after such marriage be banished and removed from this dominion forever. . . Be it enacted by the authoritie aforesaid, and it is hereby enacted, that for the time to come, whatsoever English or other white man or

woman being free shall intermarry with a negroe, mulatto, or Indian man or woman bond or free shall within three months after such marriage be banished and removed from this dominion forever.

The reading of this law might make it appear that white servants and black, mulatto or Indian slaves were choosing to marry, (or that black, mulatto, Indian and white men and women who were free were choosing to intermarry,) but remember that the law forbade indentured servants to marry without the consent of their masters. Some of the masters may have had moral misgivings about children born out of wedlock, and perhaps that would be the reason for having the black slaves and white bondservants marry. More often, the cause would have been that the wives of slaves were also slaves, as were their children. The law was specifically intended to apply primarily to interracial marriage between servants, slaves, and free people of any color.

The fact that these marriages were often not made willingly is underscored by a passage from the *Calendar of State Papers* from Maryland, 1692, in which Mary Peters, an indentured servant, petitioned the court to be freed because she had served the 8 years of her contract, but she "had been drawn by her master and mistress in to marrying a Negro," and so the court declared her a slave.

The same holds true in the case of the Maryland laws enforced in 1684, *An Act Concerning those Servants that have Bastards*, which said that any servant who could not prove who fathered the child would be held responsible for all costs imposed on her master by the birth. If the father was a servant, he had to pay half the costs. If a freeman was the father, he was responsible for the entire cost. Naturally, a woman could not name the master as the father of the child unless she had absolute proof, as he could deny it and no court would take her word over his. And it is easy to imagine that, if other servants or slaves knew that the master was the father, they would not be eager to testify to that fact. Therefore, the woman would be held responsible for the cost of the birth, and since she would be unlikely to have money to pay it, she would be required to work it off, adding time to her sentence.

Another law passed in 1692 named severe penalties for white servants having mulatto children, again, no matter if the servants were acting of their own free will, or not. The owners used these laws as well to add time onto their unpaid servants' terms of service, as, of course, it most cases they could not pay these fines, and if the child was by a mulatto slave, the child would be born a slave as well. This enabled the owners to keep the labor of the servants for even longer than they were originally sold for. According to Mellisa A. Roe in *Differential Tolerances and Accepted Punishments for Disobedient Indentured Servants and Their Masters in Colonial Courts*, the amount of time a woman servant could be expected to pay for becoming pregnant and giving birth varied between 280 and 320 days.

Her research also shows that about half the pregnant servants in Maryland whose cases she studied were ordered to be whipped as punishment, with the number of lashes ranging from 12 to 30.

It should be remembered that women servants, being either low in social class or convicts, were, by the very nature of their servitude, considered to be loose women with low morals, and therefore, no court was likely to rule in their favor against their masters, no matter what fate they had suffered. If , even today, a woman victimized by rape is often said to have been "asking for it," then these poor women were "asking for it," merely by the fact that they were in servitude.

Some colonies specified that children born of a white indentured servant and a black slave were not slaves, but they could be sold away from their mothers as indentured servants until they reached the age of 21. Obviously, many of these parents never found their children again, just as with the slaves whose children could be sold away.

Surely, the practice of "breeding " slaves helped to account for the observation of Reverend John H. Aughey, who preached to both black and white, free and slave congregations in the South for eleven years. He spoke of preaching to slaves with red hair and blues eyes, many of whom appeared as white as he was himself.

The fate of women indentured servants was a hard one most of the time anyway. Thebaud. in *The Irish Race in the Past and Present*. described those women brought to New England in the 1600's and 1700's:

Such of them as were sent North were to be distributed among the 'saints' of New England, to be esteemed by the said 'saints' as 'idolators', 'vipers' , 'young reprobates,' just objects of the 'wrath of God'; or, if appearing to fall in with their new and hard taskmasters, to be greeted with words of dubious praise, as 'brands snatched from the burning',' vessels of reprobation,'destined, perhaps, by a due initiation of the 'saints[, to become 'vessels of election,' in the meantime to be unmercifully scourged by the 'besom of righteousness' for the slighted fault or mistake.

When all of this was over, once a servant completed his time of service, should he or she survive, they were entitled to receive clothing, some land, and other items according to which colony they were in. In one account, the servant was to receive "clothing, two hoes, three barrels of corn, and fifty acres of land. *(Indentured Servants Experiences 1600-1700,*

Multicultural Activites for the American History Classroom.)

After the Revolution, the practice of indentured servitude continued to bring so many people into the colonies, that the United States Constitution actually mentioned them specifically, in Article 1, Section 2:

> Representatives and direct Taxes shall be apportioned among the several States which may be included within this Union, according to their respective Numbers, which shall be determined by adding to the whole Number of free Persons, including those bound to Service for a Term of Years.

What was life like for the typical indentured servant?

Let us take the example of those employed by the Hampton Farm and Northampton Iron Works. These properties were owned by the Ridgely family, and the papers are preserved by the Maryland Historical Society. In R. Kent Lancaster's *Almost*

Chattel, written for the *Maryland Historical Magazine* in 2000, he gives an account of information drawn from these papers. The servants worked 26 days a month, with Sundays off (although they could not leave the property without permission even on that day), and about one day a year for holiday. either Christmas or December 28[th]as a rule, although that was not always the case. They were provided with clothing made of a cheap cloth known as "slave cloth" and shoes, but, while shirts were given out two at a time, each servant received on one pair of pants, which had to last for 5 or 6 months before another pair was given, making it obvious that there could have been very little washing of clothes done during that time. The few women servants included in the records received pants, just like the men. The only difference between the women's apparel and the men's is that the women also received aprons. Clothing and shoes were bought and handed out in bulk, without regard to fit. Every indication is that the clothing was barely adequate, but rough, skimpy, and threadbare, as befitted a slave and not a free person. Part of the reason for this was to make servants and slaves who ran away easier to spot.

The descriptions of servants' food found in the papers are horrifying: Rancid beef and flour full of worms and other insects are mentioned. The main diet for the servants was pork or beef, fresh or salted, and various gruels and coarse breads of flour or cornmeal. Once in a while, they might have herring or mackerel. There were gardens on the property, so they probably had vegetables. Sweets were extremely rare indeed. The diet was limited and boring, but the servants did not starve. Drink, particularly a cheap alcoholic beverage called grogg, was plentiful. Servants were often drunk, no doubt to make life more bearable, but also because the cheap booze was in plentiful supply. Many probably became alcoholic due to drinking grogg on a regular basis, from necessity rather than from free will.

In other places, indentured servants were treated much more harshly than those owned by the Ridgely family. A bondswoman in Maryland in 1756, for instance , wrote of ""toiling almost Day and Night—with only this comfort that you Bitch you do not halfe enough, and then tied up and whipp'd to that Degree that you'd not serve an Animal." ("Lusty Beggars, Dissolute Women, Sorners, Gypsies, And Vagabonds For Virginia," By Bruce P. Lenman, Colonial Williamsburg website.)

Of course, Irish slaves and servants did not just work on the plantations.

Some of the Irish indentured servants were skilled craftsmen, and of course, craftsmen were in much demand in North America. For instance, many Irish printers were forced to leave Ireland for printing "patriotic" pieces that the Crown found seditious and dangerous, and came to America where they served out their indentures and were able to set themselves up to publish and print some of the country's earliest newspapers.

OTHER FORMS OF VIRTUAL SLAVERY AND
INDENTURE

There were occupations which used almost exclusively white, usually Irish, or Asian labor in because of the danger and hardship of the work, as black slaves were too expensive to be as disposable. Even after the term indentured servant was no longer in use, this practice continued in the form of contract labor. Thousands of Irish lives were lost building the nation's railroads and canals. There, life was so cheap that laborers who died were often buried in unmarked graves near the worksites, with no ceremony or recording of their deaths. Indeed, *Smithsonian Magazine* reported in its April 2010 issue that a mass grave containing the remains of 57 Irish immigrant workers was recently discovered in Pennsylvania. They probably died of cholera and were buried quickly and with no ceremony, covered up so that the company would not have trouble recruiting new workers. "Similar burial sites lie alongside this country's canals, dams, bridges and railroads, their locations known and unknown; their occupants nameless," said the Smithsonian article. So common was death among the railroad workers that it was commonly said that "an Irishman was buried under every tie."

During the Potato Famine in the mid-1850's, another huge wave of Irish immigrants came over, often agreeing to work as indentured servants or contract labor under whatever circumstances just to stay alive and not starve in Ireland. The Famine had been preceded by huge "clearances" in Ireland. Between 1847 and 1854, over a quarter-million people were evicted from their homes. This was the result of the "Gregory Clause," which stated that no tenant who was inhabiting more than a quarter of a acre of land was eligible for public assistance, so the Irish, who could not subsist without assistance when the potato crops began to fail because Catholics also could not hold jobs other than agriculture, were forced to turn their land over to landlords. The landlords would then evict them, often with extreme force, and burn the houses and outbuildings to the ground so that they could not come back. They then were forced to die of starvation or disease or go to the workhouses, where they were often transported, or to agree to go to America as indentured servants no matter what the circumstances of that indenture might be.. In some cases, the landlords themselves would pay for the tenants to "emigrate" on the aptly named "coffin ships," whether the tenants wanted to go or not.

These practices were not confined to the 1800's. Earlier clearances led Jonathan Swift, in 1729, to write his famous satire, "A Modest Proposal," in which he suggested using the children of the Irish poor as food:

> A young healthy child, well nursed, is at a year old, a most delicious, nourishing and wholesome food; whether stewed, roasted, baked or boiled; and I make no doubt, that it will equally serve in fricassee or ragout... I grant that this food will be somewhat dear, and therefore very proper for landlords; who, as they have already devoured most of the parents, seem to have best title to the children

This poem illustrates the plight of the
dispossessed Irish and the heartless attitude
of most of the landlords:

THE BOREEN SIDE
By James Tighe

A stripling, the last of his race,
lies dead In a nook by the Boreen side;
The rivulet runs by his board and his bed,
Where he ate the green cresses and died.

The Lord of the plains where that stream wanders
on, -
Oh! he loved not the Celtic race --
By a law of the land cast out fellow man,
And he feeds the fat ox in his place.

The hamlet he leveled, and issued commands,
Preventing all human relief,
And out by the ditches, the serfs of his lands,
Soon perished of hunger and grief.

He knew they should die -- as he ate and he drank
of the nourishing food and wine;
He heard of the death cries of the famish'd and lank
And fed were his dogs and his swine.

That Lord is a Christian! and prays the prayer,
'Our Father' -- the Father of all --
And he reads in the Book of wonderful care,
That marks when a sparrow may fall.

And there lies that youth on his damp cold bed,
And the cattle have stall and straw;
No kindred assemble to wail the lone dead –
They perished by landlord law.

He lies by the path where his forefathers trod –
The race of the generous deeds,
That sheltered the Poor for the honor of God,
And fed them with bread -- not weeds.

Unshrouded he lies by the trackless path,
And he died as his kindred died –
And vengeance Divine points the red bolt of wrath,
For that death by the Boreen side.

Because of the horror of the famine, efforts were
made to get the children, at least, to America, so
that they might live. This annotated fragment of a
letter from "Irish Famine Refugees" at RootsWeb
illustrates the situation and explained the perils of
how to get the children out:

> "... is just back from burying the children.
> Theys 3 and 20 of them dead now the
> past fortnite. Ye'll be knowin of
> O'Holeran and the Doyle families any
> day now. Morris would have bring the
> tidings. Macky and O'Connor got 27 on
> Wednesday last and Tierney took 4 and
> 10 to Kinsale [Co. Cork] to Donal H.
> [Harney], and we sent 6 more in the

tinkers cart to John and Mike S. at Cobh [Co. Cork]. We has not the way to carry many other now because they is too sick to walk any distance for certin. Any way theboots is wore off of them what has thim and thim with out is foot bludy. Ye can't be comin to get them in a cart can ye? We has the watch out for majustrats men or sheriff's peeple and there are women at the bog lanes to cry out to us. We has the better part of a keg of sprat an morsel of smelt an some of them apples from the Yankees that Willy H. [Harney] brung up to us. Pady Dardis brung a liver and lites of a ram what they downfalled on help from the hounds. Casey and Hicky come up with some cock and 2 duck and some of the lads caught some doves. If ye could find some flint or matchers fer fire makin we have need of thim also. A bate of the injin corn [Indian corn from America] could help to make the stretch of the food we have here and potion for the flux. We has not a boot amung us...

... The dead were put in the bog near the stone to rest with a prayer to their heads. In a week we'd buried 4 and 30 and 4 more on Wednesday. ... many of those with us now aren't able to get further. Their eyes are dead in their head and they have the flu so they cry with the pain.

Bannon and Dasey have come with us
this day and have brought nine more with
scurvy…"

The Irish immigrants who fled to America were
hated by many. Lodging houses turned them away
and bars and restaurants refused to serve them. If
they finished their indenture, they met signs
everywhere saying, "No Irish Need Apply."
Because of this, indentured or 'free," they had to
take the hardest, most dangerous jobs and were
treated more harshly than other servants. In the mid-
1800's a non-Irish servant wrote home to his
family," My master is a great tyrant, he treats me as
badly as if I was a common Irishman." The writer
further added, "Our position in America is one of
shame and poverty." So if this poor soul was being
treated so badly and he considers that he is being
treated as a common Irishman, one can see what
sort of treatment was generally expected for the
Irish servant.

Irish indentured servants and contract labor also did
the dangerous work of stonecutting in the quarries
to build buildings such as the Smithsonian "Castle"
and other famous American buildings. This picture

is of slaves and Irish workers in Maryland in the 1800's:

Stonecutters at Seneca Quarry

Many Irish immigrants arrived in America in the 1800's just in time to become embroiled in the Civil War. The statistics for the Confederacy are not clear, although some sources cite 40,000 Irish soldiers in the Confederate forces, but more than 170,000 are said to have fought for the Union. Many of these immigrants had not yet had time to get settled and find work before they were drafted, and others had been treated harshly and found only

"No Irish Need Apply" signs when they attempted to find employment. Despite of this, many fought bravely. The all-Irish 69th New York Regiment gained especial fame for their bravery at Bull Run, Antietam, Gettysburg and Fredricksburg in particular.

But the brave Irish soldiers are not the ones who are most remembered. The ones who are remembered are those who rioted when they realized, when the first draft was held in July 1863, that nearly every soldier being forced into the war was an immigrant, with most of them being Irish, and that nearly every non-Irish white male being called upon was paying his way out or sending a substitute. The rioting and looting that broke out when the mob's anger finally overflowed lasted for three days in cities like New York and Boston and was only quelled by armed troops returning from Gettysburg. Unfortunately, because of the years of competing for the lowest paying and most dangerous jobs and the cheapest, most undesirable housing caused free blacks to be a particular target for the rioters. Resentment between these two groups flared up time and time again in the 19th and early 20th centuries, and led to many unfortunate events in Irish American and African American history.

The song, "The Hush," expresses the deep anger and resentment that the Irish forced to fight for a cause they knew nothing about in a country they hardly knew:

It's by the hush, me boys

I'm sure that's to hold your noise,

And listen to poor Paddy's narration.

For I was by hunger pressed,

And in poverty distressed,

And I took a thought I'd leave the Irish nation.

Chorus:

So, here's you boys,

Do take my advice;

To Americay I'd have youse not be farin'

For there's nothing here but war,

Where the murdering cannons roar,

And I wish I was at home in dear old Erin.

I sold me horse and plough,

Me little pigs and cow,

And me little farm of land and I parted.

And me sweetheart, Biddy McGhee,

I'm sure I'll never see,

For I left her there that morning, broken hearted.

Meself, and a hundred more,

To America sailed o'er,

Our fortune to be making, we was thinking;

But when we landed in Yankee land,

They shoved a gun into our hand,

Saying," Paddy, you must go and fight for Lincoln.
"

General Mahar (Meagher) to us said,

"If you get shot or lose your head,

Every murdered soul of you will get a pension."

Well, in the war I lost me leg

All I've now is a wooden peg;

I tell you, 'tis the truth to you I'll mention.

Now I think meself in luck

To be fed upon Indian buck

In old Ireland, the country I delight in;

And with the devil I do say,

"Curse Americay, "

For I'm sure I've had enough on their hard fighting

Male indentured servants and contract laborers also worked, in the last years of the eighteenth and early years of the nineteenth centuries, on the canals, especially in the South and the Mid-Atlantic States. For instance, when the Erie Canal was being built in New York City in 1818, at least a quarter of the workers were Irish. Thousands of Irish men moved into Albany to do work related to the canal, and while it is not possible to know how many of these were indentured servants, it is a safe bet that many of them were, and those who were contract laborers were not much better off. These men lived in barracks and shanties and worked from sunup to sundown, with a two-hour break for dinner. Because of the nature of the work, the poverty of the living conditions, and the drinking, violence, and gambling that always accompanies these sorts of conditions, the canal workers were considered the lowest of the low and avoided as much as possible by everyone else. Even many slave owners would not allow their slaves to work on the canals, because it was too dangerous. It became a saying, according to *Ireland and the Americas: culture, politics, and history: Volume 2,* from which I have drawn these facts, that "to build a canal four things were needed: a pick, a shovel, a wheelbarrow, and an Irishman."

The conditions under which most Irish immigrant families lived who were not given shelter as part of their indenture, such as the contract laborers, were atrocious. According to Kirby A. Miller in *Emigrants and Exiles,* in the mid-1800's in Providence, Rhode Island, an average of 9 people lived in two rooms. In New York, as many as 75 people lived in12 rooms, paying $4 a month for rent. J.F. Watts, in *The Irish American,* reported that some Irish families in New York lived in hovels for which they paid $3 a month rent, overrun with rats which spread disease from the overflowing sewage in the outhouses. This took a great toll on children, with 2/3 of he deaths in New York in 1857 being children under 5, most of whom were Irish.

Some Irish indentured servants, mostly women, worked in sewing rooms. The sewing room conditions were horrible, in most cases. In *The White Slaves of Free America*, John T. McGinnis quoted a pamphlet written by "Nell Nelson" (an obvious pseudonym), in which she described the conditions in one shop where she spent a day in the 1800's. The youngest girls were 13. The average age was 15. "All the girls," ,she writes," were pale and haggard, some were very pretty, some few had color in their cheeks, but it was the hectic flush, not the healthy glow of youth and physical strength." There were also 8 men and 2 boys in the room- "poor young fellows in their teens, with mealy complexions, wild eyes, hollow cheeks, and sunken chests. Neither weighed a hundred pounds, but both pressed goods with heavy irons, and were cuffed and pushed about by the boss and his assistant. The men worked in slippers and undershirts, without straps or suspenders to keep their trousers in place, and the girls wore heavy peg shoes." They worked in compulsory silence, and were forbidden to stop, even to stretch. The workers worked from dawn to dusk, with a 40-minute lunch break at which they ate bread and drank cold coffee, if they ate or drank anything at all. This particular shop paid the workers "slave wages" of between $1-$3 a week. Indentured servants did the same work in the same conditions, for nothing other than whatever room and board their master chose to give them.

Many Irish women who were indentured were chambermaids, nannies, cooks, and performed other domestic duties which people of higher status abhorred. According to "Irish Immigrants in America during the 19th Century" on the Kinsella family genealogy web page, it was commonly said that "Let Negroes be servants, and if not Negroes, let Irishmen fill their place...", clearly indicating that the Irish could be given jobs that even the slaves were considered too good for.

Other indentured servants and immigrants, including many Irish, were so poor that they should also be counted slave labor even if they were paid a pittance. They worked in the factories. They were paid a tiny amount for dangerous and soul-killing work, if they were paid in money at all. Often, they were paid in "company script," which could only be spent in company stores for necessities such as food and firewood. The Irish song, "Rich Man, Poor Man," talks about that situation:

When you go to dinner, you have to run,

Or they'll blow the whistle before you're done.

Payday comes you won't have a penny,

When you pay your bills, cause you got so many.

The merchants they're all turning gray,

From figuring out how to get your pay.

Now some people run the mill folks down,

But cotton mill people make the world go round.

When winter time comes you'll have to pay,

You go to the boss, you'll have to say:

"I want a load of wood, a ton of coal

Take a dollar out a week or I'll go in the hole."

You have to buy your groceries at some chain store

Cause you can't afford to pay any more.

If you don't starve I'm a son of a gun, '

Cause you can't buy beans without any mon(ey).

Many of these factory workers were children.

Remember that even in the 1800's, during the Industrial Revolution, children could still be indentured from the age of 4 or 5 until they reached legal adulthood at 21. These children were at the complete mercy of the adults who owned them, and could be put to work at dangerous, grueling jobs for 12 or 15 hours a day or night, and forced to turn over any tiny wage they made to their masters, their legal guardians. Children who should have been in school were getting a different sort of education in factories and mines all over the country. Even those who were not indentured were still slaves to economic necessity, forced to work for pennies so that there families could survive.

The Industrial Revolution had created many factories and a voracious need for workers. Children as young as 6 years old were forced to work in these factories, around extremely dangerous machines, for 16 hours a day, 6 days a week. There were few or no precautions for their safety, except that women and girls were supposed to wear their hair up. Despite of this, stray curls would come loose and get stuck in the machines, causing these children to be scalped from foreheads to the back of their necks, an injury they seldom survived. Hands, arms, feet, and legs were regularly caught and mangled by the machines. There was no provision for children or adults who were injured in this way. They were put out on the street to beg or die. Their only value was their ability to work, so once that was gone of what use were they? If workers, even very young ones, were late or fell asleep, they were beaten. If they cried, they were beaten. This system existed from the beginning of the Industrial Age in the 1800's until as late as the 1920's!

Factory children

The Factory Inquiry Commission report to Parliament in 1833 indicated that children as young as 5 endured a working day of 14-16 hours, aside from breaks and meals. The report revealed that factory owners permitted overseers to flog and mistreat children and often did the flogging and mistreating themselves. In many factories children worked 12-hour night shifts. Medical reports to the Commission showed that thousands of these children were maimed for life by factory work, especially since fatigue, malnutrition and lack of sleep often led to terrible accidents.

Children were also routinely sent into mines, as they were small and could get into spaces a grown person could not. Very small children, as young as 5 or 6, were sometimes employed above ground by the mine bosses, operating the winding gear that sent the miners up and down the shaft, solely responsible in many cases for these men's safety. At 7 or 8, they went below ground, alone in the darkness. Slightly older children, boys and girls, were hitched to wagons, particularly in coal mines, and used to haul the heavy loads along tramways, underground, in the dark barely broken by lanterns.

Also, due to the fact that they were small, boys were given the dangerous job of chimney sweep, going up into chimneys to clean them out and thus prevent fires. Many children were badly burned or suffocated in this way, or later died when their lungs failed due to the constant intake of coal dust.

In 1900, the U.S. Census noted that 18.2, or nearly one in five, of the children in the country between the ages of 10 and 15 were working. This practice was not stopped until the passage of the child labor laws. The National Child Labor Committee, founded in 1904, compared child labor to slavery and said that it was just as important to do away with it as it had been to do away with other forms of slavery.

Some other places these children, many of them the children of immigrants and, in the case of the dirtiest, lowest paying jobs, often Irish, worked, included glass factories, where "boys traveled as distance of nearly 22 miles in an 8-hour shift at a constant slow run to and from ovens... average pay of 72 cents per 8-hour shift...."; soap-packing plants, where "...girls were exposed to caustic soda that turned their nails yellow and ate away at their fingers..."; "...arsenic, liberally applied to produce vivid colors, wrecked the appearance and health... with sores, swelling of the limbs, nausea... complete debility..."; and canning factories, where ""...children as young as six employed as headers and cleaners (of shrimp and fish)... stand for shifts of 12 hours and longer in open sheds... hands immersed in cold water...".(Quotes from *The Good Old Days: They Were Terrible!* By Otto L. Beltmann.

For this work, the children were paid between 3 and 5 cents an hour on average. If that does not sound like slavery to you, consider that for many of them, even that money was paid in company script, meaning it could only be used at company-owned stores or to pay rent on company-owned houses. Children and parents alike were held in thrall in a unbreakable cycle of debt and servitude in mines and factories all over the country.

While the first child labor legislation passed in 1918, it was not until 1938 when the Fair Labor Standards act passed, that the practice was effectively ended and these children were freed from forced bondage. Obviously, not all of these children were Irish, but most Irish children in America in this time period were probably among them.

Children operating factory machines

Children were not the only indentured labor sent into the mines. In the 1870's until around 1910, many Irish and Scottish men came over to America as labor gangs. In exchange for passage, the laborers signed an agreement with a contractor, who negotiated wages for them and kept a cut. The men signed willingly, not being afraid of working hard and believing that this was their way out of poverty, but they did not know that they were signing up for a life of dangerous, miserable work at little pay, with employers who had no care for their safety and cared only for their own profit. This same method was used to provide laborers for the steelyards.

A cartoon from Puck magazine, "Uncle Sam's Lodgin House, illustrates the conditions under which immigrants lived. The cartoon was not bemoaning the terrible housing conditions, but showing the Irishman as the only emigrant stirring up trouble:

Because the conditions in the mines was so horrible in Pennsylvania, the Irish miners formed a secret union called the "Molly Maguires" to combat the mine bosses who kept them and their families in slavery and treated them brutally and with careless disregard for disfigurement or death to the workers.

The Molly Maguires fought brutality with brutality. They ambushed and beat and sometimes even killed the mine bosses, who ran the mines for absentee owners. They were not educated, goal-oriented, or particularly well-organized. They simply fought back with the same methods the mine bosses used against them.

This made the 1860's and 1870's a time of unprecedented violence in the Pennsylvania mines, but it brought attention to the terrible conditions of the miners, both child and adult, and those who depended upon them. Their methods were deplorable, and led to the hanging in 1877 of 20 men, some of whom may have been innocent.

There is a famous ghost story, for instance, concerning Alexander Cambell, who declared his innocence right up until the time he was hanged, and who left a handprint on the wall of the Carbon County Jail which he claimed would stand as testament to his innocence. Despite every effort to paint over it or remove it from the wall, the handprint remains clearly visible to this day.

Despite, the regrettable nature of the actions taken by the Molly Maguires, they did lead directly to the rise of later, stronger and more legal labor unions, which led to improvements in conditions ranging from limiting child labor, raising wages, and limiting work hours to improving safety conditions in the mines, although mining never became a safe occupation and abuses continued in the industry even long after the establishment of unions and laws.

Irishmen also made up the majority of the workers on the railroads. This work was so dangerous that death was a daily occurrence, and workers were hastily buried in shallow graves along the rail embankments, while the work continued relentlessly on. The workers and their families lived in tent cities near the tracks, always ready to strike and move as the work moved. An Irish folk song of

the 1840's, "Paddy Works on the Railroad"
describes a bit of the railroad experience;

In 18 hundred and 42, I left the Old World for the
new
Bad cess to the luck that brought me through
To work upon the railway.

It's Pat do this and Pat do that, without a stocking or
cravat.
And nothing but an old straw hat
To work upon the railway.

And when Pat lays him down to sleep
The little bugs around him creep
And not a bit can poor Pat sleep
While working on the railway.

Conditions for railroad workers were so bad that
disease was rampant in the makeshift camps, and
care was virtually non-existent. The discovery of
the mass grave of 57 Irish immigrant railroad
workers in Duffy's Cut, Pennsylvania, made the
news in 2010. At first, it was thought that all of the
men had died of cholera. But further investigation
revealed that some appeared to have been shot and
others had suffered blunt trauma. In other words,
they were murdered. The theory is that when
cholera broke out among some of the Irish workers,

local vigilantes killed them all to make sure no cholera escaped the valley.

In general, the only difference between later forms of contract labor such as this, and child labor in factories and elsewhere, and actual slavery and indentured servitude, is that the children or contract workers could not be sold as the slaves could or willed as the slaves and indentured servants could, and that the children, railroad workers, miners, and other contract laborers of the sort were given some sort of "wage," though often in the case of the contract laborers, it was company "script," which could only be exchanged at company stores at prices the company set.

The contempt in which both Irish and black people were held post-Civil War, when slavery, but not indentured servitude and contract labor had been abolished, is illustrated by the words of the English historian Edward Freeman, who visited America in 1881. He wrote,

> This would be a grand land if only
> every Irishman would kill a Negro, and
> be hanged for it. I find this sentiment
> generally approved - sometimes with
> the qualification that they want Irish

and Negroes for servants, not being able
to get any other.

REBELLION

Of course, the Irish did just not meekly accept their fate, whether enslaved or indentured against their will, or tricked into signing papers that promised conditions that did not materialize, or fooled into contract work by false promises. They developed very poor reputations as servants, because they were very prone to run away or to stir up rebellion.

In a study of runaway slaves and "servants" in Pennsylvania in the years from 1771-1776 cited in Clark's book, more than half of them were Irish, and since they could speak English and they were not dark-skinned, it was much easier for them to run in the colonies than it was for the black slaves or those unfortunate white slaves in the West Indies or Barbados, who had no place to run to (but who rebelled anyway, even if it meant death or dire punishment.)

Runaway indentured servants who were captured were punished harshly, just as slaves were. They were usually beaten and often chained and if they ran away more than once, wee regularly branded. Time was always added to their service, at least equivalent to the time they were missing and usually more.

Laws were made forbidding ship captains from giving passage to runaway indentured servants, and rewards were made for their return, as illustrated at the end of this advertisement from the Virginia Gazette of 22 October , 1736 ,concerning an English servant:

RAN away the 20th of July last, from the subscriber, an Irish convict servant Man, named Cornelius McAllen, he is above a middle Stature, and well proportioned, and very dark Hair'd, between 30 and 40 Years of Age, well cloathed, and had about 4 Pounds Cash when he went away. Whoever secures him, so that he may be brought to me, in the County of Lancaster, shall be paid Fifty Shillings, besides what the Law allows,   Richard Bo...

Here is one 1642 law regarding runaway indentured servants:

Whereas there are divers loytering runaways in the collony who very often absent themselves from their masters service, And sometimes in two or three monthes cannot be found, whereby their said masters are at great charge in finding them, And many times even to the loss of their year's labour before they be had, Be it therefore enacted and confirmed that all runaways that shall absent themselves from their said masters service shall be lyable to make satisfaction by service at the end of their tymes by indenture double the tyme of service soe neglected, And in some cases more if the comissioners for the place appointed shall find it requisite and convenient. And if such runaways shall be found to transgresse the second time or oftener (if it shall be duely proved against them) that then they shall be branded in the cheek with the letter R. and passe vnder the statute of incorrigible rogues.

As mentioned earlier, Slaves who ran away more than once could be punished by being shackled or having iron collars affixed for the term of their indenture, as is illustrated by advertisements stating that the servant was wearing a leg shackle and short chain, or the case of Francis Bacon, who had run away four times and, in the advertisement for his return on the fifth try, was noted to have "also an iron collar on." (Lancaster)

In Massachusetts, the problem of rebellion among Irish "servants" was so bad that in the 1650's a law was passed that no Irish person could be imported into the state.

RAN away, on the 30th of September last, from Mr. Patrick Creagh, of the City of Annapolis, Two Servant Men: One named John Conner, a Sail-maker by Trade, much Pock fretten and freckl'd in the Face; has Red Hair and Beard, wears a Wig or Cap, is an Irish Man, and talks upon the Brogue: Had with him a dark brown Pea Jacket and Breeches, and is supposed to have some other Cloathes; He came this Year from Bristol, in the Ship Essex, Capt. Henry Morgan, Commander. The other named Ralph Taylor, a North-Country Man, is a Middle-siz'd Man, of a flow Speech, wears his Hair, which is of a brown Colour, and is a Convict: Had on a brown Coat, and Ozenbriggs Trowsers. Went away (also) with them, a Servant Woman, named Sarah Miers, a Dutch Woman, and talks broken English, pretty Tall, Round Shoulder'd, Likely in the Face, and had a flat Nose: They took with them some Wearing Apparel, viz. A dark Grey Coat trimm'd with Black, a Woman's Blue Cloak, fac'd with White Silk; a Seersucker Gown, one white Linen Ditto; one strip'd Calimanco Ditto, a brown Camblet Petticoat, a Woman's Bermuda Hat, lin'd with Blue Silk, and several other Things, viz. Bedding, Linnen, and in particular a Red Rugg. They went in an old Carvil Work Long-Boat, with one Mast, and a Square Sail. Whoever secures the said Servants, and brings them to the Subscriber, living in Annapolis, shall have Five Pounds Current Money as a Reward, and reasonable Charges: And if taken out of this Province, they shall have Six Pounds in Gold Reward, and all reasonable Charges, paid by   Patrick Creagh.

Maryland &.

RAN away, from the Subscribers, on Monday Night, being the 12th Instant, from the Town of Cambridge, on Great Choptank River, in a Long-boat belonging to Mr. Thomas Newett, having a blue Vane, with T. N. on it, the following Persons, viz. Thomas Abbrebett, of a middle stature, dark Complexion, dark Wigg, Dark-colour'd Coat turn'd ; a red Duffil Great-coat, and blue Broad-cloth Breeches. Jane Shepherd, a lusty fat Woman, having a Gold-lac'd Hat, a dark brown Holland Gown, and another striped ordinary One; also Cambrick Pinners and Handkerchiefs, with several Aprons and Shifts ; is an English Woman. Francis O'Connor, a tall spare Irish Man, being thin and poorly cloath'd, wore his own short black Hair, a Felt Hat, blue Stockings, a check'd Shirt, and had several other white Shirts, a Gun, a Remnant of coarse brown Holland, and several other Things. Mary Barnes, having a green Silk Poplin Gown, fac'd with Yellow ; a sickly Countenance, and much bloated. And Jane Harlett, a Scotch Woman having a strip'd Calimanco Gown, a Flatt Hat, and several other Things.

Whoever secures the said Persons, and Boat, so that they may be had again, shall receive of the Subscribers, Ten Pounds current Money of this Province ; or for each Person as followeth, if taken separate,

For Thomas Abbrebett, the Sum of 1 l. 15 s. For Francis O'Connor, 5 l. For Jane Shepherd, 5 l. For Jane Harlett, 10 s. For Mary Barnes, 5 s. For the Boat, 1 l. As also Reasonable Charges for all or either of them, paid by

Thomas Newett,
Thomas Watkins.

In 1765, Maryland added to their laws concerning runaway servants that :

> Sheriffs, having any Runaway Servants
> or Slaves committed to their custody,
> after One Months Notice…or Two
> Months Notice, if such owner do not
> appear within the Time limited, ..Such
> Sheriff shall set up Notes appointing the
> Time….and Place for Selling such
> Servants or Slaves…

Servants or Slaves, harbouring or entertaining other Servants or Slaves…for One Hour, or more, are punishable by Whipping, not exceeding Thirty-Nine Stripes….

The Irish slaves also conspired with the black slaves to revolt together in the colonies. In 1676, there was a huge slave rebellion in Virginia that burned Jamestown nearly to the ground. Hundreds of people died as the result of white and black slaves rebelling together. The owners, fearing that this would happen again, decided that they had to divide the slaves against each other. No longer were they housed together. New rules were enforced which denied more rights to the black slaves than the white ones. For instance, white slaves could no longer be whipped naked without a court order, as they previously could be and often were.

White slaves were given power over black slaves as overseers in many cases. Whites were also given different clothing. So, although their treatment, housing, and general situation were no better or worse in most cases, the black and white slaves were no longer united. The owners and the courts deliberately set out to create feelings of superiority on the part of white slaves and resentment on the part of black slaves so that they would not rise up together, a situation which worked remarkably well and helped to foster years of future racism and ill-will.

A better form of rebellion which actually did help many male indentured servants earn their freedom, although at quite a price, was to join the military, especially during wars such as the French and Indian War. Parliament would allow servants to enlist, and all the masters could do was hope for compensation.

Later, during the Revolution, the Congressional Congress and some of the colonies encouraged the servants to enlist, although Pennsylvania and other colonies passed a law forbidding it, which the military routinely ignored, accepting servants as recruits just the same.

PRINCE GEORGE, *Nov.* 23, 1776.

CONTRARY to my defire, and ex-
prefs order, my fervant man JAMES
BULLOCK enlifted with mr. *Robert Poy-
threfs*, an officer, he fays, under captain
Scott of the *Georgia* fervice; upon which
I demanded my fervant of the faid *Poy-
threfs*, without effect. This is therefore
to requeft of capt. *Scott* to have my faid
fervant returned to me without delay or
farther expenfe, or I fhall certainly profe-
cute him according to law.

2   JAMES ANDERSON.

In addition to these ways of escaping the terms of
indenture, sometimes other employers would entice
the servants away. They might offer to hide
servants, shorten their time of service, give them
much better conditions, or even, if the need for
labor was great, offer freedom and wages in place
of indenture. Of course, if the servant was
apprehended, he or she would be returned to their
master and punished. At the very least, extra time
would be added to the indenture period. Very often,
the servant would also be beaten, branded, or locked
up or chained for a period of time. An act was also
passed in Pennsylvania to fine any person who hid

or kept an indentured servant away from his master for more than 24 hours.

To discourage runaways in Pennsylvania, an act was passed in 1775 which required inns to question travelers:

> All unknown persons coming to lodge or sojourn in an inn, or ask for work…in any house, and cannot give a good account of themselves and their former and present way of living, and have not a pass under hand and seal of at last one Justice of the Peace, stating where they came from and their destination..shall be taken up as a suspect criminal.

Even though this act was passed in 1775, the likelihood of being questioned and accused of being a runaway existed before then, at least in the North, for Benjamin Franklin wrote of his travels between Philadelphia and New York in 1723:

> I stopped at a poor inn where I stayed all night…I made so miserable a figure that I found, by the questions asked me, I was suspected to be some runaway

indentured servant, and in danger of being taken on that suspicion.

In later years, as we have seen, the Irish fought for better conditions for themselves and their families through unionizing, in the mines, sewing rooms and factories. Often, the fights between union members and the "pit bosses" and other authority figures were long and bloody and lasted for years. But strides were made, and conditions slowly improved. Child labor laws, mandatory lunch breaks, minimum wage, and many benefits we take for granted came out of these struggles between the Irish and other immigrants and the masters and bosses. This also led to the Irish involvement in politics which eventually allowed the first Irish Catholic to become President years later, with the election of John F. Kennedy.

The Irish, though beaten and sometimes broken, as an ethnic branch of American citizens, prevailed, and became part of the backbone of this country. It is time for Irish Americans, Canadians, citizens of Barbados and the West Indies, in Australia and all around the world, to know and understand how we came here and what our ancestors suffered and how they fought to get us where we are today.

AUSTRALIA

FIELDS OF ATHENRY
By Pete St. John

By a lonely prison wall, I heard a young girl calling
"Michael, they have taken you away,
For you stole Trevelyan's corn,
So the young might see the morn.
Now a prison snip lies waiting in the bay."

Low lie the fields of Athenry
Where once we watched the small free birds fly
Our love was on the wing
We had dreams and songs to sing
It's so lonely round the fields of Athenry.

By a lonely prison wall, I heard a young man
calling
"Nothing matters, Mary, when you're free
Against the famine and the crown,
I rebelled they cut me down.
Now you must raise our child with dignity."

By a lonely harbor wall, we watched the last star
fall
As the prison ship sailed out against the sky
For she lived to hope and pray for her love in
Botany Bay
It's so lonely round the fields of Athenry.

After the American Revolution, Britain began
shipping their Irish "prisoners" to Australia rather

than America. As always, while some of these transported criminals had committed real crimes such as highway robbery, these "convicts," particularly the females, may have been convicted of stealing an apple from the market, cutting a tree on an aristocrat's land, or poaching a sheep to feed a starving family. Or perhaps a young person who strayed a bit too far from home and been picked up for "vagrancy." They were then jailed, loaded aboard a ship, and sent to a life of servitude in Australia. There was no difference made either on land or aboard ship between those picked up for minor crimes and those who had been scheduled to hang as highwaymen or murderers. Men were supposed to have been convicted of a capital crime or repeated acts of violence to be transported, but for women, it took far less. There were so few real female criminals, and the demand for women in Australia was great.

And even for men, by far the most common crime was that of stealing cattle, pigs, or sheep. For many of the Irish, their only regular food was the potato. Hunger led them to chance stealing animals for food, and that crime often carried a life sentence. The penalty was either hanging or transportation.

According to the article, "Irish Diaspora," in *Wikipedia*, 50,000 Irish men and women were transported between 1791 and 1867. Today, 33 to 40% of Australians claim Irish heritage, double the percentage of Americans who are known to have Irish ancestry. Many were sentenced to "Van Dieman's Land" for 7 to 10 years, but most remained in Australia even after their sentence was complete. (Van Dieman's Land was an island of the southeast coast of Australia.)

Many of these convicts were women and children. Indeed, according to the National Archives of Australia, about a quarter of the early convicts were under the age of 18.

Once a transportation decree was handed down, prisoners were taken to horrid, overcrowded jails such as Newgate and Killmainham in Dublin to be held until a ship was ready to take them to their new home. Conditions were minimally improved in 1817, when a new holding facility just for convicts to be transported was built in Cork, and in 1837 a separate jail was provided in Dublin for female convicts facing deportation, who had not been kept separately before then. One can only imagine the sad lot of these women before 1837, with no protection from the male convicts they were housed among. Sometimes, deportees had to wait in these prisons for up to two years before being transported. When the prisons were too full, those waiting transport would be held in "hulks," disabled ships moored along the ships. The conditions in the hulks were so dreadful that disease was rampant and those who did not die of them brought them onto the transport ships with them, so that disease was also a constant concern on the ships, with many outbreaks of typhus and cholera.

Once aboard ship, the conditions were similar to slave ships anywhere, except that the convicts were better fed, being given bread, beef, red wine, and vinegar and lime to prevent scurvy. They were kept in holds, not allowed access to the decks, and forced to sleep in chains.

In the 1820's, the Surgeon Superintendent, Peter Cunningham, described the sleeping condtions thus, as quoted in ":Irish Convicts Transported to Australia" at Rootsweb.com: "Two rows of sleeping-births, one above the other, extend on each side of the between-decks, each berth being 6 feet square, and calculated to hold four convicts, everyone thus possessing 18 inches of space to sleep in…" ("and ample space, too!" he opined.)

Although the first Irish arrived in Australia on *The Queen* in 1791, there was a great increase in the number of Irish convicts sentenced to transportation after the United Irish Rebel Uprising in 1798. These rebels were so badly treated that they rebelled again at Castle Hill in Australia in 1804, but the uprising failed. Nine of the leaders were executed. Most of the rest were beaten and sent to the Coal River Chain Gang.

In 1848, more Irish rebels, this time members of the Young Irish Party, were transported after an uprising against the British.

Not all of the Irish who ended up in Australia were political prisoners or rebels, however. Some were not convicts, but came more or less willingly, as well, especially after the discovery of first copper and then gold in the 1800's. But all of the first Irish settlers were transportees.

Once the ships landed, all free men were allowed to choose servants from among the convicts. This was done by an assignment system. Free men had to apply and provide information as to how many servants they required, how many they already had, and how much land they owned. Once they had their servants, they housed them in slab houses with bark roofs, and provided a blanket, a pot, and a knife, plus two suits of clothing a year. For many of the Irish, this was more than they had ever had at home.

The most dangerous prisoners were usually sent to road gangs, but the main need was for farm workers, so the majority of male convicts were put to work on farms. Females who were given honest employment were cooks, maids, nannies, or employed in other domestic work.

One observer, quoted in "Irish Convicts Transported to Australia", stated that the Scottish convicts were considered the worst servants, while the Irish were considered the best. This was not a matter of national character, but because of the nature of English law: "A man is vanished from Scotland for a great crime, from England for a small one, and from Ireland, for hardly no crime at all."

Irish and other children who were poor, abandoned, or orphaned were regularly sent to Australia beginning in the 1800's and until 1967 to work on farms and perform other labor. This was done with the best intentions by various charitable organizations and due to Poor Laws which allowed the government to pay to ship any children under their care to Australia or New Zealand to earn their keep there. The intention was to rescue these children from poverty and a life of crime and send them to a place where they would have better lives and more opportunities, and for many of the children it was a better situation. However, because there was inadequate supervision, many of these children were, of course, mistreated and overworked.

In 1901, the Australian Government enacted the Immigration Restriction Act, which decreed that only white people could be sent to Australia, thus insuring that there would be more Irish, Scottish and English children among those sent involuntarily to Australia since neither black nor Asian servants were allowed.

Beginning in 1903, a series of "farm schools" were set up which trained male children and youths taken from workhouses for three months before sending them out to work on farms in Australia, especially in New South Wales. Many of these were young men between the ages of 15-19 years of age.

In 1913, the Child Immigration Society of Oxford established a farm school at Pinjara, a very remote location in which, for the first few years, the children and staff struggled daily to survive. World War II ended all immigration from Great Britain, but beginning in 1920, it was reinstated and the school at Pinjarra received considerable financial assistance from the British government, as well as more shipments of children.

This system continued in operation except for brief interruptions related to wars until the last 9 children were sent to Australia as child migrants in 1967.

Of course, not only Irish people, whether children, women, or men, were shipped to Australia. Britain used the country as a dumping ground for prisoners and workhouse inhabitants of all races before the passing of the Restriction Act.

Many of the women transported to Australia actually were prostitutes. But many of the female convicts deported were sent on any trivial charge that could be mustered, or no charge at all, and once they were, there was no guarantee that they would be treated any differently than the professional prostitutes. After all, to whom would they complain? They were not fine, educated ladies.

And once they were taken aboard ship to be transported, it did not matter whether they were virgin or whore, decent or disreputable. All women of the day were considered either angels or fallen women, and convicts could not be angels.

The older women were luckier than the younger, as they were more likely to be given honest jobs and unmolested.

One observer reported in the Select Parliamentary Committee on the State of the Jails for 1819 what happened to the women as soon as they were put to sea on board ship:

These women told me...that they were subject to every manner of insult from the master of the ship and the sailors; that the master stripped several of them and publicly whipped them; that one young woman, from ill-treatment, threw herself into the sea and perished; that the master beat one of the women with a rope with his own hands, till she was much bruised in her arms, breasts, and other parts of her body...

And things did not get better for these poor women after they arrived, especially if they had been mistreated aboard ship, because then they were damaged goods and of even less value for anything other than prostitution.

In a letter, T.J. Plummer wrote to a friend in 1809 about what happened when the ships arrived. The letter was preserved in *The Historical Records of New South Wales, Vol VII*: "It will perhaps scarcely be believed that, on the arrival of a female convict ship, the custom has been to suffer the inhabitants of the colony to select one at his pleasure... as avowed objects of intercourse..."

Sometimes, there was not even a limit to how many women could be thus acquisitioned. In 1803, 40 transports of women were counted as "women allowed to the New South Wales Corps," According to Brian Fitzpatrick in *The Australian People (1788-1945)*. In other words, all these women were turned over to the military for their pleasure or to be used however the corps chose to use them.

Despite all of their troubles, the prisoners who landed in Australia gradually, as they gained their freedom, formed their own societies with their own rules, language and customs, which often still exist as part of the Australian culture today.

CANADA

Canada first came into existence as New France in 1608, when Samual de Champlain established a small colony of about 60 settlers at the location on the St. Lawrence River which is now Quebec City. While the city was French, there were a number of indentured servants who came to serve the farmers and fur traders, most often for 3 years. There were also women known as Filles de Roi ("daughters of the King,") who were sent to be wives of the male settlers, usually retired army officers. They were looked after by Ursuline nuns until they were chosen by a settler as a bride. However, these early servants and Filles de Roi were French. It was not until the 1800's that many Irish people came to Canada.

After the War of 1812, many Irish Catholics came to Ontario and worked in the same unsafe and despised positions they worked on in the States: the railroads, the canals, building roads, cutting lumber. Rather than being indentured or enslaved, however, they worked for free land, and many of them actually received the land by which they were enticed to Canada. Many others were tenant farmers, particularly around Peterborough in the 1820's.

Canada, did, however, received indentured servants, mostly from the Hudson's Bay Company, which used these servants to do the dangerous and unsafe work in the mines around Nanaimo into the late 1800's.

When the potato famine forced many Irish to leave their homes or starve, most by signing on as indentured servants or whose passage was paid by landlords eager to get them off of their land, they were brought to the American continent on ships so horrible they were described as "coffin ships." So many of these ships arrived in Canada, carrying sick and dying passengers, that a quarantine hospital complex, which consisted of mere sheds, was set up on Grosse Isle in 1846. Within a short space of time, the hospital sheds which were meant to hold about 200 people, were crowded with thousands of the sick and dying Irish immigrants.

The only people who could be found to care for these poor immigrants were, as the superintendent in charge noted, "the most abandoned of both sexes." He goes on to say that "six men are constantly employed digging large trenches from five to six feet deep, in which the dead are buried", and, according to the article "Gross Isle" in *Untold Story: The Irish in Canada*, he also is quoted as speaking of the dead being "dragged" out of the hold of ships with boat hooks. The ones who made it to shore were neglected and often robbed of what little they had by those who were supposed to care for them. No accurate account is recorded of how many Irish immigrants died at Grosse Isle, but a monument erected to them on the isle speaks of "thousands." Because most of these poor souls died and the rest were feared and rejected due to the danger of fever, very few of these Irish immigrants ever worked as servants or laborers in Canada.

Many of the tenants sent by landlords, particularly Lord Palmerston, to Canada were of no use as servants or workers at all. Palmerston's people arrived in the freezing cold on nine ships, almost all of which carried only widows, young children, the aged and the decrepit. They arrived almost naked. One woman on the first ship to arrive was completely naked and had to be wrapped in a sheet before she could leave the ship. They had been promised clothes and money when they arrived, but no clothes or money were provided. These emigrants could only become objects of charity. The citizens of St. John, New Brunswick, could not shoulder the burden of the care of those emigrants they received and offered food and free passage back to Ireland to any who would agree to go. The Council at New Brunswick sent a message to Lord Palmerston;

> …Common Council of the City of St. John deeply regret that one of Her Majesty's ministers, the Rt. Hon. Lord Palmerston, either by himself or his authorized agent should have exposed such a numerous and distressed portion of his tenantry to the severity and privations of a New Brunswick winter... unprovided with the common means of support, with broken-down constitutions and almost in a state of nudity…

In the 1840's, large numbers of immigrants did work on the Jubilee Bridge, now known as the Victoria Bridge, in Quebec. This was the first bridge to link the island of Montreal to the South Shore. Under the auspices of the Grand Trunk Railway, the Irish slaved away with little regard to their health or safety. They lived in tents at the base of the bridge, and 6,000 of them died of typhus and were buried in a mass grave that has since been unearthed.

As elsewhere, Britain found it helpful to use Canada to rid itself of some of its indigent children. In addition to Canada's own poor, who often indentured their children to landowners as farm labor or domestic help, England began shipping thousands of children to Canada as indentured servants in 1869. Not all of these children were Irish by any means. Many were Scottish or English, but there were Irish children among them. .Nationality ceased to matter once mostly well-meaning Victorians chose them to be sent to "homes" in Canada. They were labeled "orphans," but many of them did have families. They were the children of the poor, taken from workhouses, debtors' prisons, the streets, and orphanages. Over 150,000 "home children," as they were known, were shipped to Canada.

12,000 of the children went to Quebec, while
70,000 went to Ontario. There was little supervision
of the program, as usual, so the children were easy
targets of abuse until they reached the age of 18 and
their indenture ended. Some were lucky and were
treated well, even at times like members of the
family. The classic children's book, *Anne of Green
Gables* reflects the lot of these children. In the
story, an elderly bachelor and his spinster sister
decide to adopt an orphan to help with the farm.
They ask for a sturdy boy, but they get a girl
instead. At first appalled, they come to love and
value Anne, despite the many scrapes she currently
gets into.

But many of the orphans were not so lucky. The trade unions hated them, referring to them as "unwanted guttersnipes" who were stealing jobs, even though the children had never had a say in their fortunes. Even when they were not mistreated, they were often treated the same as an adult worker would have been, deprived of love or friendship from those who took them in, provided for materially as long as they did their work but not given the nurture that children usually need. While it is true that these children would probably not have fared any better at home, and might well have fared worse, their situation was often very hard.

It was in 1869 that Scottish evangelist Annie MacPherson brought her first 100 children to Ontario. Father Nugent, of Liverpool, England, began organizing the transport of Catholic orphans the same year. Since Ireland was so close, many of Father Nugent's charges would have been Irish.

In 1872, MacPherson opened two new homes in Canada to receive children, one in Ontario and one in Quebec. She began transporting children from the Smyley Homes in Dublin as well as her own establishment in London. Her intentions, of course, were to save these children from grim lives of poverty and degradation, and in many cases, she was no doubt successful. These children are included here only because the situation did cause some morally impaired people to take advantage of the helplessness of these children to overwork and abuse or neglect them.

An article from the Australian National Archives which contains a timeline of child migration states that in 1875, the chief Poor Law Inspector, John Doyle, expressed grave concerns about child immigration in Canada. As a result, fewer children were sent from workhouses, reformatories, and industrial schools and more were sent from private orphanages and charitable foundations, which would presumably be more careful to insure their care and safety.

According to an article in the Ottawa Citizen, February 24, 2010, entitled "An Apology from Home," John Sayers of British Isles Family History Society of Greater Ottawa, estimates only about 5% of the children were really abused. These include a 15-year-old named George Green who died in 1895 in Ontario, apparently of beating and starvation. His master was acquitted on charges of manslaughter. The article goes on to say that suicide was common among home children. The girls, of course, had the worst time of it. Most of them were around 17 and many of them were molested by those who were to take care of them.

Even among those children who were not molested, loneliness and confusion were terrible problems. They were torn from their families and they did not understand why: What had they done wrong? Little attempt was done in most cases to explain the reasons why they were brought to Canada, even to the youngest ones.

As everywhere else, some indentured servants, including these children, were treated fairly, and some were not. In some cases, conditions were very harsh, and Canadian servants ran away just as those in the colonies and in the West Indies and Barbados did, although perhaps less often.

An example, from the article "Indentured Servants" by June Payne Flath in *Country Connection Magazine*, Summer 2005, is of a sixteen year old girl named Jane Ralston, who happened to be Scottish, who was indentured as a domestic servant in Upper Canada in the 1850's. She was very unhappy, so when the opportunity arose, she ran away. Because she was European in appearance, she was able to avoid recapture and made her way to Niagara Falls, where the article tells us she "married Samuel Hall, a black fugitive slave from the American south. Together they operated a hotel in the Niagara Falls district and provided carriage transportation for tourists."

In general, however, it must be noted that those Irish who survived the journey to Canada and did not die in quarantine were more likely to successfully assimilate and subject to less mistreatment and prejudice than they experienced in the U.S. , unless they worked in the mines. Many of the adults were fishermen, loggers, and other rugged outdoor workmen who were only expected to work hard but not to conform to the rules of urban society. Their different ways, their religion, and their language were no burden to them in the frozen North. And the children were, in general, better provided for and trained so that when they reached adulthood, they could enter the general population and support themselves.

"FREEDOM"

What Happened to Those Who Did Win Their way to Freedom?

That depended on where they were, but in all cases they eventually assimilated if they lived.

In 1633, the island of Monserrat became a colony. Her governor, Anthony Brisket, encouraged Irish "servants" who had managed to survive and serve their time to come there and settle, since most were forbidden to return to Ireland even if they had had the funds.

By 1680, there were twice as many Irish on Monserrat as English. There were a number of Irish governors, and for a while, the former slaves prospered, growing tobacco on small farms. But then, in the mid-1600's, sugar began to replace tobacco as the main crop.

This was disastrous for the small farmers, because sugar cannot be grown on small farms but requires large plantations. Some Irishmen managed to raise the funds necessary, but most were relegated to the jungle slopes where they barely managed to eke out a living from agriculture. The plantation owners brought in slaves, both African, and, ironically, indentured Irish. In 1678.of the 2,682 whites living in Monserrat, 1,644 were bonded or indentured, creating a vicious circle. Since 70% of the population at that time was Irish, it follows that over 1,000 of these indentured servants were no doubt Irish as well. And a small percentage of those were owned by other Irishmen who had once been slave themselves.

However, eventually the practice of indentured servitude was abolished, and the former slaves either became assimilated into the culture or moved on to the colonies, where they established themselves with more or less success.

In the colonies, indentured servants who survived and served out their term were usually given "Freedom dues," using including clothing, a gun, and a small portion of land. Most of these former slaves eked out barely enough to live on, but some did prosper. Many moved on to other areas, and settled there. Skilled workers were more fortunate than the unskilled labor. A few actually managed to rise from poverty to wealth, but these were very few indeed. Others settled into at least comfortable circumstances. Many remained laborers, share-croppers, factory and dock workers, miners, and in dire cases, vagrants drifting from place to place.

What became of the women is less well-documented. Obviously, the women were not given land. It can be assumed that most of them married; those who did not would have remained in service, doing similar work, probably, to what they were doing before, except for a wage instead of for free, and with at least a little more freedom of choice than they had had before.

After the Civil War, the Irish began to take on new and somewhat better occupations, although they were still often dangerous and underpaid jobs. The Irish had a near-monopoly on the newly created jobs of policeman and firefighter, for instance, and are still represented more than any other ethnic group in those professions. As horsecars and streetcars became popular near the turn of the 20th century, the Irish not only laid the tracks for them but many of them became the first drivers and conductors. By 1900, the Irish made up about a third of all the plumbers, boilermakers and steamfitters in the United States. The Irish became involved in the Unions early and that led to much political involvement. Many also sought careers in the Catholic Church as nuns and priests. In all these ways, through hard work, perseverance, politics, and the Church, the Irish advanced in America.

In Australia, as we have noted, the indentured servants and convicts who did their time and won freedom created their own unique society with its own rules and ways of speaking, many of which are still a part of Australian culture today.

In Canada, assimilation was made easier by the nature of the work and the geography. In less urban areas, it was easier for the Irish immigrants to blend in and find their place in the less industrialized fields of logging, fishing, and agriculture.

In the long run, of course, most of the Irish in America, Canada , Australia, and the West Indies were absorbed into the mainstream of life, with no stigma attached to their former status. The majority of Irish-American, Canadians .and Australians today, while proud of their Irish heritage, may not even be aware that their ancestors worked as slaves and servants to gain them their heritage, while in the West Indies and Barbados, the Irish element of the island histories have added obvious and colorful threads to the cultural patchwork.

AFTERWORD

It is my hope that this book will fill in missing pages from the history of the Irish in the West Indies, America, Canada and Australia. It is also my hope that it will broaden our understanding of the nature and history of slavery and involuntary servitude, making it less of a racial issue and more of a human one.

Today, in many parts of the world, slavery still exists, as does indentured servitude. In even more places, contract labor still holds many people virtually slaves. Even in America, immigrants, particularly those from Mexico and other Spanish-speaking countries, work illegally in sweat shops and dangerous or undesirable jobs in terrible conditions and for inadequate pay. Even those who enter the country legally are often treated with the same contempt my Irish ancestors may have faced, accused of taking work from Americans and treated with resentment and contempt in many cases. Human rights are not a thing of the past, even in the so-called civilized country, and perhaps a better understanding of the past will help us see and recognize the patterns and somehow learn to break them.

In any case, this book is offered as a testament of love and respect to those Irish men, women, and children, who worked hard, suffered much, and either lived or died so far from their native land.

BIBLIOGRAPHY

Linebaugh, Peter & Rediker, Marcus: *The Many-headed Hydra: The Hidden History of the Revolutionary Atlantic*. Boston: Beacon Press, 2001.

Karras Ruth Mazo: *Slavery And Society in Medeivel Scandinavia.* New Haven: Yale University Press, 1988.

Connelly, James: *The Reconquest of Ireland*. Sioux Falls: NuVision Publications, LLC, 2007.

Sowell, Thomas: *Ethnic America.* New York: Basic Books, 1981

Miller, Kerby: *Emigrants and Exiles: Ireland and the Irish Exodus to North America,* New York: Oxford University Press, 1988.

Miller, Kerby A. (Editor), Schrierm Arnold (Editor), Boling, Bruce D. (Editor), Doyle, David N. (Editor): *Irish Immigrants in the Land of Canaan: Letters and Memoirs from Colonial and Revolutionary America.* New York: Oxford University Press, 2003.

Woodham-Smith, Cecil: *The Great Hunqer; Ireland 1845-1849.* New York: Penguin Group,1992.

Macmanus, Seumas: *The Story of the Irish Race: A Popular History of Ireland (1922).*New York: Cornell University Library, 2009.

Metlzer, Milton: *Slavery: A World History.* Cambridge: Da Capo Press, 1993.

Williams, Joseph J : *Whence the "Black Irish" of Jamaica.*Lincoln MacVeigh/The Dial Press, 1932.

Lenihan, Maurice: *Limerick, its history and antiquities; ecclesiastical, civil, and military,from the earliest ages, with copious historical, archaeological, topographical, and genealogical notes.* Nabu Press, 2010.

Akinson, Donald H: *An Irish History of Civilization, Volume 1.* Montreal: McGill-Queen's University Press,2006.

Jordan, Don and Walsh, Michael: *White cargo: the forgotten history of Britain's White slaves in America.* New York: NYU Press, 2008.

Renwick, W.L. and Spencer, Sir Edmund: *A viewe of the present state of Irelande, 1934 Edition.* Native American Books Distributor, 2007.

Emmet, Thomas Addis: *Ireland Under English Rule*.Whitefish: Kessinger Publishing, LLC, 2007.

Purvis, Thomas L: *A Dictionary of American History*. Wiley-Blackwell, 1997.

Hayden, Tom: *Irish on the Inside: In Search of the Soul of Irish America*. New York: Verso,2003.

Miles, Rosalind: *The Women's History of the World*. Topsfield: Salem House Publishing, 1992.

Clark, Dennis: *The Irish relations: trials of an immigrant tradition*. Madison: Fairleigh Dickinson University Press, 1982.

Mittelberger, Gottlieb: *On the Misfortune of Indentured Servant*: 1754.

Crimmens, John Daniel: *Irish-American Historical Miscellany: Relating Largely to New York City and Vicinity, Together with Much Interesting Material Relative to Other Parts of the Country*. Whitefish: Kessinger Publishing, LLC, 2007.

Annu, Ogu Eji Ofo (editor): *White Slaves in Americas*.

Thebaud, Rev. August J: *The Irish Race in the Past and Present*. Whitefish: Kessinger Publishing, LLC, 2010.

Coleman Philip, Byrne, James, & Kling, Jason (editors): *Ireland and the Americas: culture, politics, and history: Volume 2.* Santa Barbara: ABC-CLIO, 2008.

McEnnis, John T: *The white slaves of free America: Being an account of the sufferings, privations and hardships of the weary toilers in our great cities as recently exposed ... child labor, contract and prison labor.* R.S. Peale and Co., 1888.

Bettman, Otto: *The Good Old Days: They Were Terrible!* New York: Random House, 1974.

Fitzpatrick, Brian: *The Australian People (1788-1945).* Santa Barbara: Greenwood Publishing, 1982.

O'Driscoll, Robert & Reynolds, Lorna (editors): *Untold Story : The Irish in Canada.* Celtic Arts, 1988.

Made in the USA
San Bernardino, CA
05 August 2013